SECRETS OF THE RARE COIN AND BULLION BUSINESS

from a Lifelong Trader

2021 Edition

MICHAEL GAROFALO

Copyright © 2021 CDN Publishing, LLC

All rights reserved.

Published in the United States by Greysheet™ Publication,
a registered trademark of CDN Publishing, LLC
1072 Laskin Road, Suite 202, Virginia Beach, Virginia 23451

www.greysheet.com

The Library of Congress Cataloging-in-Publication Data
is available upon request.

ISBN: 978-1-7342239-7-2

Author	Michael Garofalo
Publisher	John Feigenbaum
Editor	Patrick Ian Perez
Graphic Designer	Sam Crow

First edition: November 2021

Printed in the United States of America

2 0 2 0 9 3 1 8 3 4

SECRETS OF THE RARE COIN AND BULLION BUSINESS

from a Lifelong Trader

For my daughter, Jessica, my son-in-law, Alex, and my two grandsons, Elliot and Miles, as a way to remember that as much as I loved this hobby and devoted my life to it for many decades, my love for you is even greater!

CONTENTS

FOREWORD   xi

PUBLISHER'S NOTE   xii

ACKNOWLEDGMENTS   xiii

01 | WHAT IS THIS AND HOW MUCH IS IT WORTH?   17
- a. Bullion Items
- b. Semi-Numismatic Items
- c. Numismatic Items
- d. Premiums and Rarity
- e. Certified Coin vs Raw Coin Pricing
- f. Cost Plus

02 | HOW DO I PRICE THIS THING?   33
- a. eBay as a Pricing Source
- b. Check the Red Book
- c. Dealers' Websites
- d. The Greysheet
- e. CPG® Coin & Currency Market Review
- f. Online Dealer Exchanges

03 | WHAT ABOUT THESE OTHER SOURCES OF PRICING?   43
- a. Coin Magazines
- b. Numismatic Auctions
- c. Collectors Corner
- d. PCGS Coin Price Guide
- e. NGC Coin Price Guide
- f. Coin World Coin Values
- g. Summary of Other Pricing Sources

04 | OTHER FACTORS AFFECTING PRICING — 53

    a. Strike
    b. Luster
    c. Provenance
    d. Toning

05 | THE IMPACT OF ONLINE MARKETPLACES AND CERTIFIED COINS — 63

    a. Numismatic Technological History
    b. A Force in Print and Online
    c. Certified Coins in Demand
    d. Collectors Corner – Is Actually for Dealers
    e. CoinWorld Marketplace
    f. Facebook Groups (The Wild West)

06 | THOUSANDS OF ONLINE SELLERS — 77

    a. The Do-It-Yourselfer
    b. The Royal Treatment
    c. The Big Enchilada – The eBay Platform
    d. eBay For Buyers – It's Scary Out There!
    e. Know YOUR Dealer
    f. The "Twilight Zone" Known As Facebook

07 | ALL ABOUT APMEX – A DIFFERENT KIND OF ONLINE SELLER — 89

    a. In The Beginning…
    b. What's So Great About APMEX?

08 | BLACK SWAN EVENTS — 101

    a. What the Heck is a Black Swan Event?
    b. Another Pearl Harbor
    c. A Man's Home is His… Albatross
    d. You Can't Sell What You Don't Own
    e. You Want How Much?
    f. How to be Prepared
    g. Buying through the D-C-A Method

09 | TO CAC OR NOT TO CAC? — 113

    a. What in the World is CAC?
    b. A Short History of Certified Coins
    c. An Idea is Born

10 | WHAT COLLECTORS & INVESTORS NEED TO KNOW — 129

    a. Knowledge is King!
    b. What Should You Collect?
    c. Read it – Learn it – Remember it – Buy it
    d. Learn to Grade
    e. Select Your Dealer Like Your Coins – Carefully
    f. Join the Club!
    g. Record Keeping, Budgets, Insurance, Storage
    h. Buying at Coin Shows
    i. Should you Buy Coins at Auction?
    j. How to Negotiate Better Prices

11 | TO DEAL OR NOT TO DEAL? — 151

    a. 10 Rules for Being a Successful Coin Dealer
    b. Preparing for Coin Shows
    c. Coin Show Checklist
    d. Security Considerations
    e. Before the Show
    f. Traveling to the Show
    g. At the Coin Show
    h. Returning from the Show

A FEW FINAL THOUGHTS… — 169

FOREWORD

I first met Mike Garofalo in 2008 when he came to Oklahoma to interview with my company. He already had 30 years of experience as a coin dealer when I met him, and I knew hiring him would be beneficial for everybody.

In the early years we learned quite a bit from each other, and he helped me grow APMEX in ways I hadn't envisioned.

When Mike told me he was writing this book, I couldn't have been more excited for him. He has always been generous in sharing his knowledge and experience and this book is no exception as it's full of information every collector and investor should know and have access to.

More importantly than learning more, this book will encourage readers to explore their hobby further and see how they can get more involved in the coin industry. I encourage everybody to read this book cover to cover to see all the ways you can enjoy this hobby for the rest of your life—just like I have!

Thank you.

Scott Thomas,
President and Founder of APMEX

PUBLISHER'S NOTE

As the title implies, "Secrets of the Rare Coin Business" is all about shedding light on many of the complicated aspects of the numismatics trade that would otherwise be impossible to learn without years of exposure to the trade. The business of collectibles has undergone rapid change over the past several decades thanks to the Internet, but never as quickly as the past several years. After centuries of dealers and collectors doing business face to face and over the phone, the buying and selling of numismatics has evolved in ways not previously considered. Online auctions, marketplaces, and trusted web sites have become massively influential, and a new generation of dealers are constantly imagining new, more efficient ways to profit.

It is with this backdrop that Mike Garofalo has generously offered to explain the underpinnings of our business. He's taking you back stage in a rare look behind the opaque curtain. Whether you are a seasoned collector, bullion hoarder, hard asset investor, or aspiring collectibles dealer this book is required reading. Mistakes in this business can be costly but they are avoidable, and "Secrets" will steer you clear of them.

I hope you enjoy this book and we look forward to your feedback so we can continue with updated future editions to keep up with the rapid changes of the rare coin marketplace.

Numismatically yours,

John Feigenbaum
CEO and Publisher of CDN Publishing
john@greysheet.com

ACKNOWLEDGMENTS

First, let me state that the opinions expressed in this book are mine and mine alone, and do not reflect the opinions or views of any other person or company. Also, I tried to provide you will with good advice but this is not a legal guide or blueprint to follow. These are simply common sense opinions expressed after years of experience. No guarantee is implied to obtain these results and you agree to hold the author and contributors harmless on their advice.

The idea behind this book was to take the mystery out of why coins, currency and bullion items are priced in a certain manner and at a certain level. For collectors and investors this book will, hopefully, help them recognize a "good buy" and avoid a "bad buy." For new dealers starting in this business—welcome—and hopefully this book will give you some ideas and explain what may not be obvious.

There are lots of people who directly or indirectly contributed to the production of this book. First I would like to thank John Feigenbaum,

Patrick Ian Perez, Sam Crow and the staff of the CDN Publishing. John graciously shared ideas, pricing, access to their data and publications and, most importantly, critiques of chapters. Then John, as you can see, actually published it. This book would still be an idea if he hadn't believed in this project. Without his assistance, this book would never have been published.

Coin dealer and long-time friend, Andy Seminerio, provided me with insights on the Certified Coin Exchange and his view of the business over the last 45 years. Likewise, Jim Carr, another coin dealer and great friend, provided me with his insights from many years in the coin business. Tom Caldwell, a well-known name in this industry and yet another good friend, also offered his thoughts and ideas. One additional dealer who has been a powerhouse in the world of numismatics and also my close friend, Kevin Lipton, contributed to the thoughts espoused here. Finally, a true visionary in the coin business and a great friend Greg Hannigan offered his thoughts and advice to help all of you. Thanks to all of you gentlemen for your assistance.

Coin industry thought-leader and certified coin pioneer, John Albanese, provided tremendous insights into certified coins and CAC. John was there at PCGS's earliest days, started NGC and then started CAC. He has revolutionized our coin hobby by himself.

Likewise I truly want to thank Scott Thomas and the staff of APMEX for their invaluable assistance. Many of the images used in this book were courtesy of the staff at APMEX. Scott provided assistance and encouragement as I retired from APMEX to write this book and to write others. Scott also provided critical editorial assistance to me during the creation of this book. He also gave me some opportunities to lead at APMEX that were great for the Company and for me and are incorporated into my views in this book. I would like to thank MC Garofalo—no relation actually—no really—MC is a marketing genius and she was great reading this manuscript and she gave me some great ideas and visual assistance.

I would like to thank my dear brother, Frank Garofalo, who didn't live long enough to see this book come to fruition. He was my guide into the world of numismatics back in the 1960s, when we were both just kids. Over the next 50 years, Frank blazed a path that I followed into the hobby a few years later, and as I went my own way, he still provided lots of encouragement and sage advice. My foray into this great industry was made easier for me by my brother.

Most important of all, I would like to thank my dear wife of more than 40 years who has been my love, best friend and partner throughout all that time—Barbara Garofalo. She also gave me a great deal of encouragement and has truly been my stabilizing influence over that time period too. And I incessantly badgered her to be my proof-reader, another of her many and varied talents, to make certain that my stories and lessons were more entertaining than boring for you—dear readers.

Mike Garofalo

01 | WHAT IS THIS AND HOW MUCH IS IT WORTH?

How do dealers price coins to make them attractive to you, but also make some profit for themselves, ensuring that they stay in business? Well, it isn't rocket science! But you have to know at least these three things:

1. What type of item is it that needs to be priced—what type of coin or currency item is it and what is it's state of preservation (grade)?
2. What did you pay for it?
3. What does the current market believe that this item is worth in that grade?

There are a number of other factors that affect value but let's start with these. If you know what you have, it is one of these three items. It is either bullion, semi-numismatic or a numismatic item. Let me explain what these are so you will understand the differences.

BULLION ITEMS

There are three different types of bullion. A bullion item is a **Round**, a **Bar**, or a **Coin** made of gold, silver, platinum or palladium. A **Round** is a piece of precious metal that has a specific weight and purity and is made by a private company. It is usually round in shape. It is not made by a sovereign Mint. No denomination will appear on a Round.

(The well-known Engelhard Prospector Silver Round. Date, weight, fineness, but no denomination. Photo courtesy of APMEX.)

A **Bar** is a piece of precious metal that displays a specific weight and purity. It can sometimes display a date. Bars are usually made by a private company but some well-known mints make their own bars—the Royal Canadian Mint for example also makes and markets bars. Bars are usually rectangular in shape but not always.

(Royal Canadian Mint 10 Oz Silver Bars. Displaying weight, fineness but no denomination. Photo courtesy of APMEX)

A **Coin** is a metallic piece of actual money that was minted by a sovereign government—like the United States Mint or the Royal Canadian Mint. They are often round in shape, but not always. They must always bear denominations as they are Sovereign Coins. They are Legal Tender coins in the country that struck them but the value is meaningless, in that the bullion value is greater than the legal tender value. For example, a one ounce American Silver Eagle coin has a One Dollar, Legal Tender value. You could take it to a bank and deposit it into your account and be credited for One Dollar, but the bullion value (today) is around $17.00 so that would not be a prudent thing to do. But because it is a coin of the issuing country it is always backed by the full faith and credit of the issuing country. That is why legal tender bullion coins are always popular with collectors and investors.

(A 2020 American Silver Eagle coin, displaying weight, fineness, date and denomination. Photo courtesy of APMEX)

Bullion items are usually purchased as a hedge against inflation, or as an investment. They are sometimes collected, but the real value is in the actual amount of precious metal that they contain. Its price fluctuates with the movement of the precious metals price in the bullion market—minute to minute when the market is open.

So then, how is it valued? It is generally valued by prices set by the London Bullion Market Association (LBMA). The LBMA sets prices (called the "GOLD FIX") twice a day for gold and once per day for silver, platinum and palladium. This is what dealers call SPOT price. That means if gold has a spot price of $1,600.00, the underlying metal is worth $1,600.00 per Troy Ounce. But in order to buy it the Sovereign Government that minted it would charge the spot price ($1,600.00) and a premium of a few additional dollars to cover minting costs and marketing. The mint might charge $1,625.00. Now the dealer who buys it direct from the Mint needs to make a profit so he charges $1,650.00 making $25 for himself. If you do not buy it from that dealer buying it direct from the Mint, then each dealer adds a small profit to the cost of the coin, for himself, and now this one Troy Ounce of Gold is now worth $1,700.00! ($1,600.00 + $25 + $25 + $30 + $20 = $1,700.00). The price you pay OVER the spot price is called the **PREMIUM**.

```
GOLD $1,645.00  ▲ $11.10   SILVER $14.62  ▼ ($0.13)   PLATINUM $734.60  ▼ ($5.40)   PALLADIUM $2,283.00  ▼ ($3.70)
```

(APMEX displaying current SPOT prices like a Wall Street "ticker". Courtesy of APMEX.)

Who is determining these SPOT prices then? No one country, organization, or dealer, no matter how large, controls the price of precious metals. So no one can manipulate the prices. Even the LBMA is only **reporting** the prices. Wall Street investors buy millions of ounces of bullion daily, but so do investors in Shanghai, in Moscow, in Dubai, in New York—all around the world.

In addition, many of the hundreds of millions of shares of "paper" gold (think ETF's and Gold Pools) are backed by physical gold. Some world currencies use gold ownership to bolster their actual paper currency value. China strongly encourages its citizens to buy physical gold for their retirement and they discourage exporting gold out of China. In Indian cultures, gold jewelry rather than coins or bars is the preferred way of owning gold. But they trail only the Chinese in their personal consumption of physical gold.

Unlike stocks or bonds, gold doesn't pay any dividends or interest. So why do people buy it? Bullion is a tangible, hard asset. Gold has been a source of value for over 5,000 years. Bullion helps an investor diversify their portfolio. How? Well, bullion provides "insurance" for stock portfolios. It tends to go up when the stock market goes down. In that regard, it is a non-correlated asset—which means it doesn't mirror the stock market but moves opposite to it. Volatility drives people to buy gold and silver.

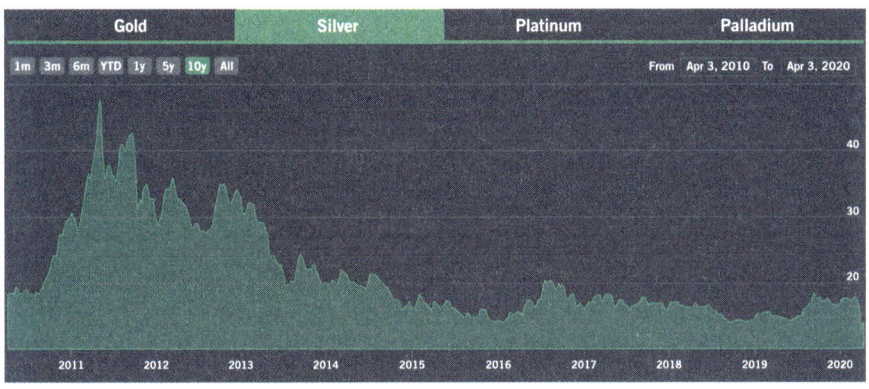

(An APMEX Silver Spot Chart displaying 10 years of volatility 2010–2020. Note a $47.00/Ounce price in 2011 and current price under $20.00/Ounce. Chart Courtesy of APMEX.)

Unlike paper assets (stocks, bonds, mutual funds) the value of bullion can never go down to zero. People buy it when they fear uncertainty in the stock markets. People buy it when they fear inflation. They buy it when they want a diverse basket of holdings. Gold and silver are "non-correlated assets"—when the prices in the stock market go down, the metals prices tend to go in the opposite direction.

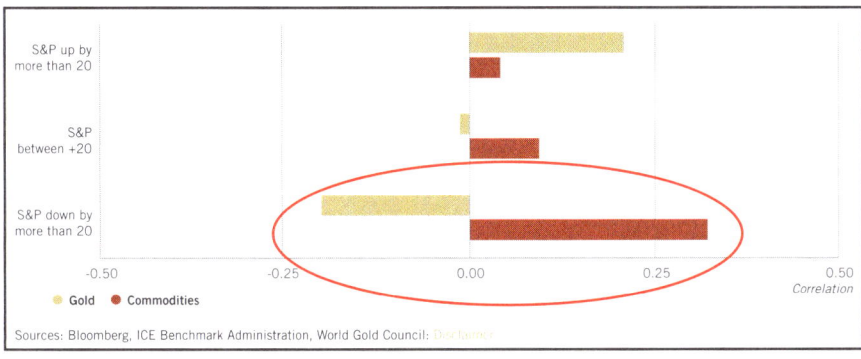

(World Gold Council chart demonstrating that Gold is non-correlated to the stock market, especially when the market drops. Chart courtesy of World Gold Council.)

SECRETS OF THE RARE COIN AND BULLION BUSINESS

During the Mortgage Crisis and Recession of 2007–2009, the stock market dropped 40%—gold went from $700 in 2007 to $1,980 in 2011 and silver went from $6 an ounce to $49 an ounce over that same time period. Stock market volatility is good for bullion prices. Worldwide economic instability is good for bullion prices. Gold is truly a long-term play. It should be held a minimum of 3 years. The higher that bullion prices go, the smaller the bullion premiums become and vice versa. Bullion comes in sizes to fit every budget from 1/10th gram (311 to one ounce) to 100 ounces (gold, platinum, and palladium) or to 1,000 ounces (silver).

- Some additional reasons that people buy bullion are:
- Bullion is private—no one knows you own it except the dealer and people that you tell.
- Bullion can be handed down to the next generation and no one knows they have it.
- Only certain types and amounts of bullion are reportable on a 1099 when they are sold.
- Hard assets are items like bullion, diamonds, fine art, antiques. The most liquid of all of these is bullion.
- Gold, especially, is recognized everywhere around the world.
- A troy ounce of gold carries just about the same value in the United States, or in China, or in India, or in Africa or anywhere in the civilized world.
- Gold and silver are essentially "universal currencies"—they have value everywhere on Earth.

SEMI-NUMISMATIC ITEMS

Okay so what are semi-numismatic items? "Semi-Numi" items are those which start off as bullion item—like American Silver Eagles—but whose value has increased due to a collectability factor coming into play. Take this example—a 2020 American Silver Eagle is not a rare item. While the final numbers are not yet known the mintage will be in the millions! Everyone wants them and seemingly, most every dealer has them. It is truly a bullion item—worth approximately $20. Now look at a 1996 American Silver Eagle. It is worth THREE TIMES that price! It has the same amount of Silver in it; it was made and distributed by the U.S. Mint just like the 2020 version. Is it the age of it? No. 1986 American Silver Eagles were the first year of mintage and they are a decade older than the 1996 version. But a 1986 coin is worth $30. Why?

MINTAGE! In 1986, the U.S. Mint struck 5,393,005 American Silver Eagle coins. But in 1996 the production of 1996–dated American Silver Eagles dropped to only 3,603,386 coins—the lowest annual production number for the entire series. Supply and demand! Everyone who collects American Silver Eagles wants and needs one. The supply is satisfying the demand at three times the price of a truly common Silver Eagle. In 2017, the U.S. Mint struck 47,000,000 Silver Eagles, the highest amount of the entire series.

So Semi-Numi coins are those with bullion content but also have a collector value that is added to the bullion value and the premium when you try to purchase it. There are literally thousands of examples of Semi-Numi coins. Many collectors and investors like them because their price generally tends to go up (due to collector demand) which can offset the up and down movements of strictly bullion coins.

There are many new coins with low or limited mintages that are being struck every day. These coins immediately qualify as "Semi-Numi" if they are made of precious metal and not only are they sold at over their bullion value, but there is a ready and willing market to buy low mintage coins. There are a growing number of issues that meet these qualifications of bullion content and lower than normal mintages. In fact many Pacific Island countries (Niue, Palau, Papua New Guinea, Tokelau, Tonga, Tuvalu and Vanuatu to name just a few) have agent companies who strike coins under the auspices of those countries but most of their coinage is sent away for foreign consumption and not for actual use within their territories. While this may seem unusual a number of these Pacific Island countries do so to encourage a revenue stream to bolster their economies.

(2018 2 Tala 1 Ounce Silver Coin from Samoa. With a limited mintage of only 30,000, which is very low for a 1 oz silver coin, it qualifies as a Semi-Numismatic offering. Photos courtesy of APMEX.)

NUMISMATIC ITEMS

Numismatic items are coins and currency, from any country around the world that has a value that greatly exceeds the item's actual precious metal value, if it has any whatsoever. Obviously currency, copper cents and the like have no intrinsic bullion value.

Some things to remember about numismatic items in how they differentiate from bullion or semi-numi products:

- Numismatic items have collectible value; most bullion items do not.
- They may or may not contain gold, silver, platinum or palladium.
- They could also be made of paper, copper, nickel or other non-precious metals like aluminum or bronze.
- Unlike bullion items, numismatic items' value is not determined by the spot price of any precious metal.
- Numismatic prices are determined by supply and demand. The greater the demand, the smaller the supply, the higher the price.
- The value of numismatic items may be great and in the millions of dollars. Or it may be low, just above face value. It doesn't matter. They are all still numismatic items.

Numismatic Items are old or rare coins or paper money. They may be issued by the United States, foreign countries or ancient civilizations. They could also be privately issued tokens or medals. Technically, **Numismatics is the study of old or rare coins or paper money.** People have collected coins since Ancient Roman times and it is an increasingly popular hobby today due to the proliferation of new issues and the information available for free on the internet.

Coins and currency are widely collected in the United States and this hobby is especially popular in many European and Asian countries. Numismatic items are valued by supply and demand and by the item's state of preservation. Prices are published on the internet and in certain numismatic publications. Prices are also realized by selling coins at major auctions. Many transactions for coins take place over the web.

Numismatic items are valued based on three important criteria:

1. **Rarity** – How scarce is this particular item? How many were originally minted? How many likely survived based on grading service population reports or their availability on the web or at coin shows?
2. **Condition** – What is the typical grade of these items? Is this coin unusually well-preserved? What is the exact condition of this coin? Even common coins may have dramatically increased value based solely on condition. These are called "condition rarities" but more on that later!
3. **Demand** – Are people collecting this particular item? Is there adequate supply to meet the demand? Are these items popular and increasing in demand and price?

Numismatic item prices are not greatly affected by the price fluctuations of silver and gold. They are more influenced by supply and demand and the state of preservation of the item in question. They are more stable than bullion generally is. But their volatility is slower generally.

Let's look at some types of very popular numismatic items.

From left to right: 1885 Morgan Dollar, rainbow toned, PCGS graded; a 1909-VDB Lincoln Cent; a 1910 $5 Indian Gold; a 1913 Buffalo Nickel; and a 1926 Oregon Trail, PCGS graded, with spectacular toning. Photo courtesy of the author.

Left to right, top to bottom: A 1977-A $1 Federal Res Note, offset printing; 1865 $2 City Bank of New Haven obsolete note; 1864 $5 State of Alabama obsolete note; and a 1775 Colonial Note for 3 Pounds from the Colony of New Hampshire. Photos courtesy of the Author.

PREMIUMS AND RARITY

Premiums are the prices you pay over the bullion value (for bullion), or over bullion value and original markup (for semi-numi) or over cost (for numismatics). It is the amount of profit that the seller is asking for in order to sell the item to you.

All sellers need to make a profit, or they are not in business for long. But the amount of profit that they make is dependent upon how scarce or common the item for sale is and how greedy or realistic the seller is.

Listed in the chart below are TYPICAL PREMIUM percentages for relatively common items in three states of rarity. Prices charged in excess of the percentages MAY indicate overly aggressive pricing. However, other factors may influence pricing such as unusually strong strike and details, attractive and original toning which enhances the appearance of the coin or the provenance of prior ownership of the coin.

Rarity Scale:
- Generic – The most common of dates and mintmarks of any type of item.
- Scarce – Not the most common items, some are a bit difficult to find.
- Rare – Difficult to find in any grade; rarely seen

Item	Generic Premium Percentage	Scarce Premium Percentage	Rare Premium Percentage
Common Bullion Items – Gold	2%	4%	10%
Common Bullion Items – Silver	4%	8%	20%
Common Bullion Items – Platinum & Palladium	6%	10%	20%
Semi-Numi Items – Gold	5%	8%	12%
Semi-Numi Items – Silver	7%	12%	25%
Semi-Numi Items – Platinum & Palladium	10%	15%	25%
Numismatic Items – Gold	8%	15%	30%+
Numismatic Items – Silver	10%	16%	30%+
Numismatic Items – Platinum & Palladium	12%	16%	40%+
Numismatic Items – Currency	15%	25%	50%+
Numismatic Items – Exonumia	20%	30%	50%+
Numismatic Items – Ancient Coins	20%	30%	50%+

Remember, scarce or rare coins will carry higher premiums due to their rarity. This applies to the majority of instances. The above percentages are only guides as to rarity and premiums added.

One additional factor is supply and demand. Something may be prohibitively rare and yet not command the amount of premium as another item might. That is frequently dependent upon the available supply of something and the requested demand for it. Even scarce or rare items may be so scarce or rare that there is limited interest in a particular thing.

Knowing what is "hot" or popular in the current marketplace is important just as is knowing what is out of favor and cannot meet the suggested premium.

CERTIFIED COIN VS. RAW COIN PRICING

Generally speaking, certified coins are worth more than raw coins. Why is that? Well when the time comes to sell your coins, whether you or your heirs do it, having the coin certified virtually eliminates any room for discussion about the grade, which translates to the value of the coin. It also removes any doubt as to the coin's authenticity.

Having your coins certified by either the Numismatic Guaranty Corporation (NGC) or by the Professional Coin Grading Service (PCGS) means that a team of experts has agreed as to the grade of your coin. Then the coin is sonically-sealed in an airtight holder with numerous anti-counterfeiting measures to protect your coin and its value. But not all coins are appropriate for certification. Some are too inexpensive while other coins have little or no premium for certified vs. raw coins.

 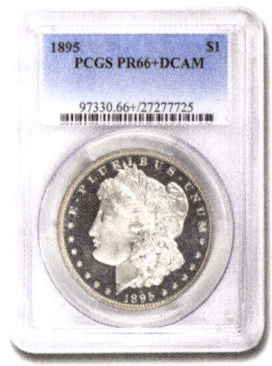

(An NGC-graded 1907 $20 Saint-Gaudens High-Relief $20 [left], an 1895 Morgan Silver Dollar Cameo Proof [right]. Photos courtesy of APMEX.)

WHAT IS THIS AND HOW MUCH IS IT WORTH?

The premiums on the chart on the prior page are applicable for coins that have been certified. These are premiums that are charged in excess of the GREYSHEET price (more on the GREYSHEET later).

The only companies that are reliable and appropriate for certification are NGC (www.NGCcoin.com) or PCGS (www.PCGS.com). While there are dozens of other companies using similar sounding names, buy only NGC or PCGS graded coins for your peace of mind. Likewise, there are two reliable certification services for currency. Paper Money Guaranty (PMG) (www.PMGNotes.com) is a subsidiary of NGC and offers reliable and consistent paper money grading. Additionally, PCGS Banknote Grading (PBG) (www.PCGS.com/banknote) is a subsidiary of PCGS and offers similar PCGS protections and guarantees.

(A PMG Graded 1918 $1,000 Federal Reserve Note [top], and a PCGS graded 1905 $20 Technicolor Gold Certificate [bottom]. Photos courtesy of APMEX.)

COST PLUS

There is one additional method of pricing that is very simple and still in use by dealers of a certain age. This method developed many years ago when pricing of coins was not the science that it is today.

If you go back in time to the 1960s, dealers would buy coins offered to them based on the Blue Book values indicated. Then they would sell coins at the Red Book published prices. So if you bought a coin at a certain price level, there may not be any indication of any price movement for a year—or more. The "Cost Plus" method works well for something that does not change in price very often.

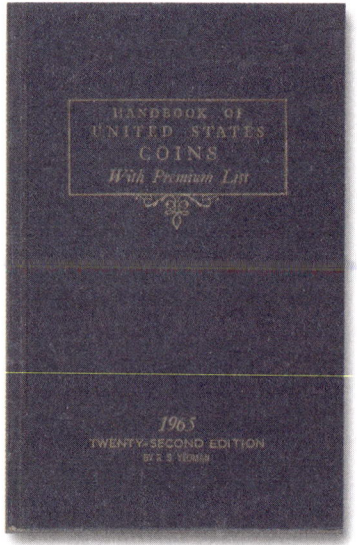 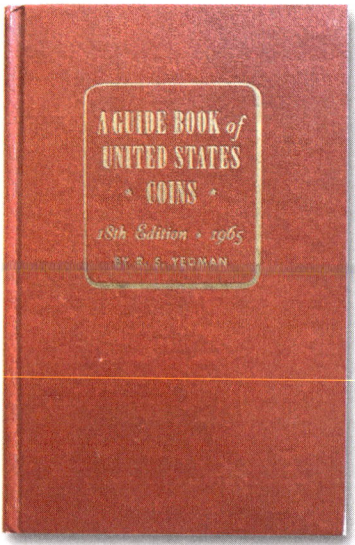

(1965 Blue Book – Handbook of U.S. Coins [left] and 1965 Red Book – Guide Book of U.S. Coins [right]. Photos courtesy of the Author.)

Some dealers eschew the pricing guides and online pricing and simply price their inventory at their original cost for the item in question and a premium representing their profit on the coin. While that is a simple solution for the dealer, it may put you, the buyer, in an unfavorable position.

If the dealer bought the coins at advantageous prices then you can likely buy them favorably. However, if the dealer overpaid for the coins because he liked them, or was unaware of prevailing market conditions, then you are at risk.

Knowing which dealers operate on a "cost plus" basis can be very beneficial for you. When they buy coins in a rising market and have bought them favorably, you may reap the benefits as well. In declining or stagnant markets—watch out. You can easily get buried in a coin. Whether the selling dealer found the coin on the sidewalk for free or paid a million dollars for it, his cost should be irrelevant for you. All that truly matters is the end cost of the coin to you in relation to where the market is for that coin, date, mintmark and grade.

02 | HOW DO I PRICE THIS THING?

Okay so you have a coin, or piece of currency (we will discuss pricing bullion later) and you want to find out what it is worth. Where do you start?

Where can you get unbiased, honest pricing of items? If you go to a dealer's website, you're going to see his retail price. Well, isn't that good enough? Can't you price it at the same level and be perfectly okay? You might be. Or you might not. Your coin might be the same date, mint mark and grade. But maybe his coin is incredibly well-struck? Or maybe his coin has "killer" bullseye rainbow toning. Or maybe he has 25 of them in stock and is dying to sell any his at a fire sale price. Or maybe he overpaid for it when the market was much higher and he is waiting for that collector who desperately needs one to stumble across his and he will get "un-buried" from it.

The answer is—you don't know! So relying on someone else's price might not be the right thing to do. You need to deduce the correct price given the current market. You can add a profit to your cost but is your cost relevant? Did you overpay to acquire? Did you buy it from someone who didn't know the price when he sold it you? Where is the market today? Did it go up or down?

EBAY AS A PRICING SOURCE

I know! I will just look on eBay! That is simple enough! There are 1,186,035 U.S. coins listed as of today. This must be the best place to find true pricing of coins.

Suppose you have an 1881-CC Morgan Silver Dollar, graded by either PCGS or NGC as MS66. There should be one price for that coin right? Let's look on eBay and find our price on a Buy-It-Now listing for a nice brilliant coin. Here is one. It is NGC graded MS66. It doesn't have toning to increase the price and it is priced at $3,350.00 or Best Offer on a Buy-It-Now listing. That has to be the correct price, right?

(An 1881-CC Morgan Silver Dollar graded MS66 by NGC listing on eBay [May 16, 2021]. Photo from eBay, Inc.)

Oh, wait a minute, there are (at the time of this search) 23 coins listed that are 1881-CC Morgan Silver Dollars, graded as MS66 by either PCGS or NGC. So as I sort the list from most expensive to least expensive, guess what I see? I see another Buy-It-Now coin, same date, same mint mark, same grade and the same grading service. Is it priced close to $3,350.00? Well, not exactly. Here is the coin at the other end of this search:

HOW DO I PRICE THIS THING?

(Another 1881-CC Morgan Silver Dollar, graded MS66, this time by PCGS listing on eBay [May 16, 2021.] Photo from eBay, Inc.)

The exact same characteristics, date, grade, mintmark and graded by one of the two premier grading services, but it is priced **$1,950.00 LESS** than the first coin. Both are Buy-It-Now coins. Both listings even say "or Best Offer" meaning that they will consider a lower bid than their asking price. What gives? Why is one coin 139% MORE than the other? What is the TRUE price? At what level should you be pricing your coin?

Frankly, if all you have is eBay to go by, you are stumped! Is this coin worth $3,350? Or $1,400? Or some other price? Which price is correct? eBay is very helpful for esoteric items, but even there, prices can vary wildly. It is a guide, but it is NOT the solution!

CHECK THE RED BOOK

The simple answer is to check the Red Book! The Red Book is "A Guide Book of United States Coins for 2020". This annual book is considered a "bible" for coin collectors. Dealers use it—a lot! I keep mine on my desk all the time and use it almost every day. It has been published annually since 1947, so it has to be the best pricing source. Right?

The 2020 Red Book values an 1881-CC Morgan Silver Dollar in MS66 grade at—wait

(The 2020 Issue of the Red Book – A Guide Book of United States Coins. Photo courtesy of Author.)

35

a minute, there is no price! Why? Well, if you read the introduction in the Red Book it states that coins priced at or over $500 are assumed to be for 3rd-Party graded coins, like PCGS coins. But it only prices coins in certain grades and it doesn't price coins over MS65 grade at all. So the Red Book is useless in helping you value your 1881-CC Morgan Silver Dollar in MS66 PCGS grade. So now what is the right price?

	Mintage	VF-20	EF-40	AU-50	MS-60	MS-63	MS-64	MS-65	PF-63
1880CC, All kinds	495,000								
1880CC, 80 Over 79, 2nd Reverse (b)		$220	$285	$350	$500	$600	$1,000	$2,000	
1880CC, 8 Over 7, 2nd Reverse (a)		210	285	325	550	600	1,000	2,000	
1880CC, 8/High 7, 3rd Reverse (a)		210	275	325	500	575	700	1,550	
1880CC, 8/Low 7, 3rd Reverse (a)		210	275	325	500	575	700	1,550	
1880CC, 3rd Reverse		225	260	325	500	575	700	1,000	
1880O, All kinds	5,305,000								
1880O, 80/79 (a)		40	65	75	200	500	2,000	16,000	
1880O		40	42	45	90	350	1,250	14,000	
1880S, All kinds	8,900,000								
1880S, 80 Over 79		30	60	65	75	150	175	450	
1880S, 0 Over 9		35	75	85	125	200	250	550	
1880S		30	33	39	45	50	65	120	
1881	(984)...9,163,000	30	37	45	53	80	125	450	$3,000
1881CC	296,000	400	425	440	475	495	550	750	

(The 2021 Red Book listing for Morgan Silver Dollars – Page 238.)

Well we have ruled out eBay as a good pricing source and we have also seen that the venerable Red Book cannot help you with this coin. I mentioned that I use the Red Book almost every day and that is a true statement. But I can use the Red Book for rarity, or to find the designer's name, or a brief historical bio about the coin or the series. But not for pricing. It doesn't provide all of the prices you are likely to need to price coins. In fact, looking at the Morgan Dollar chart above, it doesn't provide pricing for a wide variety of grades. For example, on the most widely collected U.S. coin series—Morgan Silver Dollars— there are no prices for VF25, VF30, VF35, EF45, AU53, AU55, AU58, MS61, MS62, and MS66 or higher grades. The Red Book is a useful tool, but it has its limitations. And pricing is one of its limitations.

DEALERS' WEBSITES

So where does this leave us now? Looking on dealers' websites will give you high and low prices for that same coin depending on how well the dealer is doing, their profit margins, what their cost was and a litany of other intangible factors that do not help you accurately price your coins. Is the dealer trying to make a huge margin? Are their expectations realistic? How do you know? The answer is—you don't!

But there is a third-party source that publishes unbiased pricing. They do not buy any coins. They have no coins to sell. They have no "dog in the fight" so to speak, so if the price goes up or down from month to month, they do not benefit in any way. This is the true pricing that YOU need to understand where the market is for a particular coin, in a particular grade at this point in time. **This source should be your starting point for pricing most any U.S. coin or currency item in any grade.**

THE GREYSHEET (AKA THE COIN DEALER NEWSLETTER)

The Greysheet (www.greysheet.com) is a monthly publication that has been around in various forms since 1963. The Greysheet provides pricing for nearly every United States coin as well as modern Chinese issues and other select world coins. The current monthly version comprises data that was previously distributed weekly and monthly to dealers, collectors and investors for decades.

(The April 2020 issue of the CDN Monthly Greysheet. Photo courtesy of Greysheet.)

It currently prices 31,906 individual coins and provides 236,161 prices for those 31,906 coins in a variety of grades. It is the most complete wholesale pricing guide available today. Yes, it doesn't cover everything, but it does cover most things and it continues to expand its coverage month after month, year after year.

What does the Greysheet say about our 1881-CC Morgan Silver Dollar in MS66? Does it display a price for our coin and in the specific grade?

(The Greysheet listing for Morgan Silver Dollars, April 2020 Issue, Page 87. Chart courtesy of Greysheet.)

Yes, it does! The Greysheet displays the current wholesale price in MS66 grade as $1,025.00. Remember the prices on eBay? The low price was $1,175.00 and the high price was almost $1,965.00. At the low price, the seller had marked the coin up $150.00 over "Bid"—a possible margin of 14.6%. That is a reasonable margin for a scarce coin like the 1881-CC Morgan Dollar in MS66. On the high-end, the coin was priced almost $940 over "Bid" for a possible profit margin of almost 92%! So which coin would you rather buy as a collector, investor or dealer? Which coin do you think would sell the quickest?

This is why pricing is important to you both as a buyer and as a seller. What is the likelihood that the $1,175.00 priced coin will sell? Personally, I think it is a nice coin at a great price. And again, personally, I do not think that the coin priced at almost $1,965.00 has any chance to sell.

Correct pricing determines YOUR success as a buyer and also as a seller. If you buy coins at the right price you can sell them later at the right price and still make a profit. If you spend too much initially, you either have to hope the market increases for your specific coins or the market goes up overall. Or, unfortunately, you wait for a buyer who hasn't done his homework and you sell coins to him at too much money.

If you are a collector or investor, it is even more critical to buy coins that are reasonably priced. Coins are a great hobby that provides hours of enjoyment to millions of people. But EVERY collector or investor wants to someday sell their coin collection at a profit. Whether you sell your coins to the local coin shop or your heirs sell them through a major public auction, the end result is that you hope to sell that coin that you carefully bought 30 years ago for more that you paid for it. That is what everyone wants and it is not impossible to achieve that outcome. But in order to do that you must be patient and willing to look for not only the right coin, but you must look for the right coin at the right price. Not everything you purchase will make money, but if you are careful and have some time on your side, your chances of success are pretty good. In fact, the more cautious that you are in shopping for an attractive coin at an attractive price, the more you will guarantee you (or your heir's) future success.

CPG® COIN & CURRENCY MARKET REVIEW

The CPG® Market Review is the complete listing of retail prices based on the Greysheet wholesale values. The CPG® Market Review allows retail customers to review retail pricing data from a variety of reliable sources. The retail pricing is more accurate and reflective of the current marketplace because it is so recent. Unlike other retail pricing, which may only be updated annually, the frequency and multiple sources assure much greater accuracy for the wide variety of U.S. coins and currency covered. First published in 2019, the CPG® Market Review helps collectors and investors know what to expect when buying a coin or currency item. If they find an accurately graded item

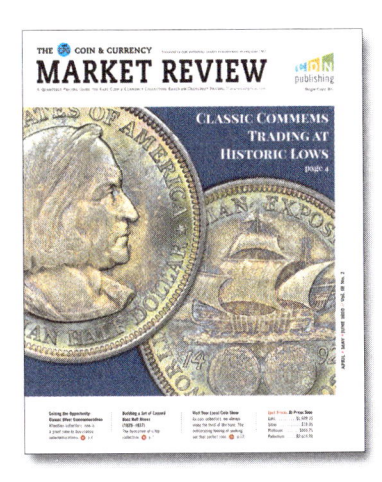

(The Quarterly CPG® Coin & Currency Market Review of Retail Pricing. Photo courtesy of Greysheet.)

at a price lower than what is in the CPG®, they can rest assured that it is a good deal and fairly priced. In this myriad of pricing options, that is a great comfort to have by your side.

Again, here is a consistent, independent, source of reliable third-party retail pricing information that is seemingly up to date and factual. Let's look at our 1881-CC Morgan Silver Dollar in PCGS MS66 as to how the CPG® calculates a retail price for it.

CPG® (Retail) Guide Value for: 1881-CC	CPG Retail Value
1881-CC MS66	
$ 1,210.00	

Greysheet® (Wholesale) Guide Value for: 1881-CC	GREYSHEET Wholesale
1881-CC MS66	
$ 945.00	
Show Price History	

Bluesheet® (Wholesale Sight-Unseen) Guide Value for PCGS-Certified: 1881-CC	PCGS Wholesale Value (Sight-Unseen)
1881-CC MS66	
$ 900.00	

Bluesheet® (Wholesale Sight-Unseen) Guide Value for NGC-Certified: 1881-CC	NGC Wholesale Value (Sight-Unseen)
1881-CC MS66	
$ 900.00	

(Chart Courtesy of www.greysheet.com)

The Greysheet Wholesale bid is $945.00. The calculated retail (CPG®) price is $1,210.00. The margin of $265 is 28%. If you look back at the table of Margin Premiums on page 14, the Scarce Coin Margin Premium begins at 15% and the Rare Margin Premium for a "Numismatic Item—Silver" begins at 30%; so this 28% margin is right within those parameters.

The 1881-CC Morgan Silver Dollar saw 296,000 coins struck. That means it has one of the lowest mintages of any Carson City Silver Dollar, including the "rare" 1893-CC which saw 677,000 coins struck. Even with the lower mintage of the 1881-CC, there are more survivors, hence the lower price. But the premium over the wholesale price is in the correct range.

THE ONLINE DEALER EXCHANGES

There are two major online trading exchanges where dealers create and execute bids and ask prices for certified coins—Certified Coin Exchange (CCE) and the CDN Exchange (CDNX).

CCE is a sight-seen and sight-unseen trading platform for coin dealers. Begun in 1990, CCE boasts over 500 dealers participating. There are over 100,000 bid and ask prices on CCE and trading is permitted on PCGS, NGC, ANACS and ICG-certified coins. There is also a dealer-to-dealer messaging system. It is owned by PCGS.

CDNX is owned and operated by the Greysheet. It is a business-to-business platform where its dealer members can post bids and asks in order to trade NGC and PCGS certified coins. Its dealer members include large auction houses and many of the nation's largest dealers. Dealers pay a monthly fee for digital access and they, too, have a private member messaging system. The CAC company posts their buying bids for CAC-approved coins on the CDNX system.

Sight-seen bids for coins tend to be higher to significantly higher as you can see what you are buying before you pay for it. Sight-unseen bids for coins are lower since your bid could be met (hit) with all kinds of coins that are mediocre for the grade or have unattractive toning or marks.

Both of these systems report recent prices realized at auction from many of the major auction houses—Heritage, Stack's Bowers, Legend, David Lawrence, Kagins and others. These "auction comps" are important pricing factors, especially for rare or unusual coins that are not often traded at coin shows or in dealer's inventories.

CDNX also offers access to all of the CDN family of pricing publications (Greysheet, Greensheet, etc.) visible on the screen to make bidding and asking decisions quick and easy. Later this year, CDNX will also release an inventory management system for their member dealers.

Below is a screenshot of the data on the CDN Exchange for the 1881-CC Morgan Silver Dollar. You can see that the populations in various grades are displayed as are the populations of the CAC-approved coins in various grades. Recent auction results are displayed as well as Greysheet and Bluesheet prices. The NGC retail price guide price is shown and there is a convenient link to a coin, in that grade, available for sale, should it exist.

(Screenshot for an 1881-CC Morgan Silver Dollar live bids and auction comps – Courtesy of CDNX.)

03 | WHAT ABOUT THESE OTHER SOURCES OF PRICING?

So we have already covered the Red Book, the Greysheet, dealer's websites, numismatic auctions, the CPG® guide, and online dealer trading networks—CDNX and CCE. That surely is an exhaustive list of pricing sources. Well, not quite.

There are other numerous sources out there to offer pricing of coins and currency. Let's review a few sources to analyze their effectiveness.

COIN MAGAZINES

Walk by any large assortment of magazines and you will certainly see a number of magazines devoted to coin collecting. These magazines have great stories about coins and collecting and terrific advice and tips, especially for novice collectors.

These are excellent magazines to buy to read and enjoy. There are great stories about interesting coins and topical stories about how what is happening in the news affects coins and coin prices. And much of the magazine covers pricing. But is it accurate and current pricing? Well, not exactly.

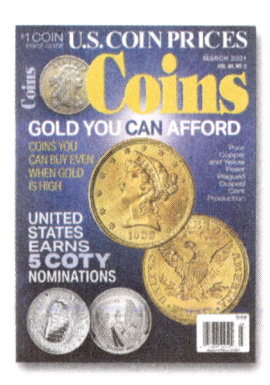

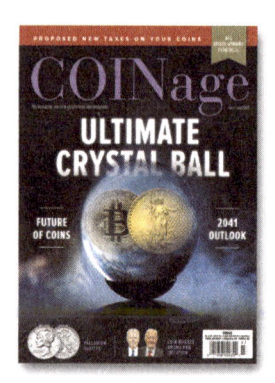

(Coins Magazine, Published by Active Interest Media. Coinage Magazine, Published by Beckett Media.)

The prices are not listed in all grades and remember magazines have publishing deadlines months in advance of their actual printing. So the prices, which are gleaned from limited sources, are already a bit "stale" by the time the magazine hits your newsstand or mailbox. They try to be accurate and they try to be current but the magazines have "ink on paper" limitations—they can't cover every coin in every grade and the prices are a tad old.

NUMISMATIC AUCTIONS

Numismatic auctions are important venues for rare and expensive coins. The average coin (< $500 in value) is more likely to be sold at a coin show, on a website, or eBay, than it is to be auctioned. Why? The cost for auctioning a coin is significantly more substantial than it is to simply offer the coin on eBay. Most auction companies charge a fee to the consignor to place their coin in auction. It costs money to photograph it, write all of the catalog descriptions, print thousands of copies and distribute it across the country. They also charge the winning buyers in auctions a fee above what they bid.

WHAT ABOUT THESE OTHER SOURCES OF PRICING?

Most auction companies charge 15% to 22% as an auction house commission, to be paid by the consignor of the coins. It is called the consignment fee. Now those rates are negotiable and if you only have a few expensive coins to sell it is easy to convince the auction house to reduce their rates. It is not unheard of that an auction house may reduce your consignor's fee to zero! And in certain cases for good customers, the auction house may pay you a fee in excess of what someone bid on the coin. They are, in reality, sharing the fee that the bidder will pay to them in excess of the hammer price.

Because of these fees, common coins do not do well in auctions. But scarce or rare coins usually do extremely well in auction because there is generally strong competition for this "fresh' material. Collectors and dealers are all competing for the same coins in a public auction. Prices realized can be very important in helping you to determine the value of the coins in question.

The major numismatic auctions houses are:

- Stacks Bowers – www.StacksBowers.com
- Heritage Auctions – www.HA.com
- Legend Auctions – www.LegendAuctions.com
- Kagins Auctions – www.Kagins.com
- David Lawrence Rare Coins – www.DavidLawrence.com
- Goldberg Auctions – www.GoldbergCoins.com

These are the major companies that share their auction records on their websites and also on CDNX and CCE.

There is another major numismatic auction house, but their data is only available on their website:

- Great Collections – www.GreatCollections.com

So as you can see, numismatic auctions are an important part of the numismatic information community but only for scarce or rare items rather than for the "average" coin. One other thing to remember is that when looking at a price realized at auction, one must also take into consideration the timing of the auction. When the auction occurred, what did the coin realize in that sale versus what the price guides stated the coin was worth? Was the coin market strong at that time? Was that coin in demand at the time it was auctioned? So many questions—but so few obvious answers!

In Coinage, for example, there are prices for 8 different grades from Very Good-10 to Mint State-65. So our 1881-CC Morgan silver dollar is NOT priced anywhere

1878-1921 MORGAN DOLLARS								
	VG10	VF20	XF40	AU50	AU55	MS60	MS63	MS65
1878-S	25	30	40	45	50	60	80	400
1878-CC	100	125	150	175	225	300	500	1750
1879	25	30	40	45	50	60	80	800
1879-O	25	30	40	50	70	100	225	4000
1879-S	25	30	40	50	55	60	100	400
1879-S (reverse of 1878)	25	30	40	80	125	200	600	6000
1879-CC	160	300	800	2250	3000	4000	8000	-
1879-CC/CC	160	300	600	2000	2500	4000	7500	-
1880	25	30	35	40	45	55	75	800
1880-O	25	30	35	40	45	75	450	31750
1880-S	25	30	35	40	45	55	70	200
1880-CC (80/79, flat breast)	650	725	825	875	925	975	1500	4000
1880-CC (8/7)	600	675	775	825	875	925	1000	2800
1881	30	-	40	-	45	55	85	800
1881-O	-	-	40	-	45	55	80	1550
1881-S	30	-	40	-	45	55	75	200
1881-CC	385	415	435	450	475	535	685	950

(Coinage, April/May 2020, Page 41, Beckett Publishing.)

in the magazine. The prices we reviewed tend to be on the "High Retail" side of pricing. But if the market has moved up or down since the publishing deadline it is NOT reflected in the published price. If you love reading about coins, a discount subscription is a great deal—look for discounts online. One company even offers a digital version of Coinage so you don't have to wait for your printed copy to be delivered.

Coin magazines may be fun to read but they should not be your reliable source for current pricing.

COLLECTORS CORNER

CollectorsCorner.com is a website run by Collector's Universe. It allows PCGS Authorized Dealers to have a website to advertise their coins. You can put in a date and grade of coin and up pops a list of dealers listing that coin for sale. But purchasing on this site is awkward, for if you find a coin that you like at a price that you like, you can place the coin in your shopping cart and when you want to check out you are directed to the listing dealer's website. Usually you will receive a call from the listing dealer and determine the best payment method for you both. You cannot actually check out on the CollectorsCorner.com website.

But as you can see, the prices range from a low of $1,175.00 to a high of $1,525.00 for that 1881-CC Morgan Dollar graded MS66 by PCGS. Which price is correct? If you are looking to price your coin how do you know that even the lowest price ($1,175.00) is correct and not too high or too low? The reality is—you don't know!

There are lots of U.S. coins available for sale and a wide range of prices from the 100+ coin dealers listing there but it doesn't really help you price your coins.

PCGS COIN PRICE GUIDE

If you search the PCGS website (www.PCGS.com/prices) you will find the PCGS Price Guide. This free service from PCGS provides retail pricing on all PCGS graded coins. In fact, there are prices in all grades and in plus (+) grades as well. It is a treasure trove of PCGS pricing.

However, again the prices tend to be "High Retail" but coins are priced in all grades. One often-heard dealer complaint is that these prices are not adjusted quickly for markets on the move, so the price that you see may be well behind the current market.

There is a "SHOP" feature which attempts to match the coin in question with the same coin for sale on eBay. But their search engine matching leaves something to be desired. My search for an 1881-CC Morgan Dollar in MS66 turned up dozens and dozens of listings of 1881-dated Morgan Dollars. Some were "CC" mintmarked but there were also "S" mints, "O" mints and no mintmarks. It really isn't as good as simply going to the eBay website and searching for yourself.

The price on the PCGS Price Guide (www.PCGS.com/price) from Collectors Universe for an 1881-CC Morgan Dollar graded MS-66 by PCGS on 5/10/20 was $1,250.00.

But there are prices for virtually all PCGS-graded coins. The pricing for the 1881-CC Morgan Dollar graded as MS66 is as follows: Again, these prices do not help you value the coin but they are an indication of what a "High Retail" price for that particular PCGS graded coin will likely be. You should be able to buy this same scarcer, but not rare coin, at lower levels on eBay and at coins shows.

NGC COIN PRICE GUIDE

Likewise NGC offers a pricing guide on their website as well (www. https://www.ngccoin.com/price-guide). But, of course, this price guide offers pricing only for NGC graded coins. The prices offered appear to be "Very High Retail" pricing.

It offers a similar eBay Shopping feature just like the one on the PCGS website. When I searched it for 1881-CC Morgan Dollar in MS66, I only received a list of 1881-CC Morgan Dollars but what was listed was in every grade imaginable. But there were no 1881-dated coins that were not from the Carson City Mint. That was an improvement over what the PCGS search engine offered.

The price for an 1881-CC Morgan Silver Dollar, graded as MS66 by NGC was $1,400.00.

One important feature that makes the NGC Coin Price Guide more valuable, in my opinion, than the PCGS price guide is the line underneath the coin listing. For the 1881-CC it states "Updated: 8/16/2019" so you can judge for yourself how current and how valid the prices actually are. PCGS does not offer similar information so you are on your own as to determine the validity of the displayed price in the current market.

Like the PCGS prices, they are listed free on the NGC website, but looking at a price that may have been valid 21 months ago is helpful in a very limited way.

Both grading services are offering their pricing as a service to their customers and the numismatic world in general but how helpful are these prices when they display "High Retail" prices that may be up to two years old. But pricing is not their actual business, grading coins is and both grading services prices should be used as a preliminary guide only.

Relying on either of their pricing guides could prove very costly were you to buy coins at these levels or attempting to sell them at comparable levels. As a dealer this is helpful information when trying to price your coins for retail sale, but less helpful for purchasing your coins at wholesale.

COIN WORLD COIN VALUES

Coin World is the oldest coin newspaper still in existence; but it is hardly a newspaper any longer. When I was a kid in the 1960s, this weekly newspaper would have more than 100 pages of stories, news and advertising—tons and tons of coins for sale. I added numerous coins to my burgeoning collection through answering ads in Coin World. But this has changed too!

Today Coin World is a slick and sophisticated glossy magazine. Gone is the black type that would often stain my fingers as I read it on the old newspaper. But also gone are the 100+ pages in every issue. Now Coin World comes weekly in the new format. The average number of pages in these weekly issues is 30+. Once a month, Coin World issues a Monthly Issue which also features U.S. coin prices, world coin prices and U.S. currency pricing. At 152 pages, (the April 2020 issue) it contains a lot of valuable information.

The Coin World "Coin Values Price Guide" covers more than 65,000 U.S. coins. It is published monthly and the prices are also available at www.coinworld.com. The prices here tend to also be "High Retail" prices which, as a dealer, do not help you price your coin for wholesale sale.

The Coin World price online and in print for an 1881-CC Morgan Dollar in MS66 is $1,250.00.

Coin World states that their pricing comes from actual transactions, public auctions, fixed-price lists and other sources. A wide array of prices is listed for each coin covered. Depending on the popularity of the series and how well collected it is, you will see more or fewer prices. All series of coins listed seem to have either 10 grade prices or 20 grade prices, depending on how well-collected they are. For Peace Dollars, there are 10 prices listed from G4 to MS65 and there is also one price in Proof grade. For Morgan Dollars, twenty separate prices are listed. Prices range from G4 to MS66 with four Proof grades also included.

This information may be helpful to you in pricing your coins for retail sale, but as for being a dealer needing to know how to price your coins wholesale and then retail, it is of limited retail value.

SUMMARY OF OTHER PRICING SOURCES

We reviewed two coin magazines—*Coins* magazine and *Coinage* in this chapter. Both have their limitations and neither presents wholesale pricing. Both present a dated and limited view of retail pricing. Neither would be helpful to you in determining whether to purchase a coin or not, or what to charge in order for it to sell wholesale. But they could be useful for retail pricing to customers. Print magazines do have limitations.

We also reviewed the website—www.CollectorsCorner.com—as a possible pricing source. Again, you are only seeing the various levels of retail pricing from more than 100 dealers. If they want to sell their coin, they must be competitive in pricing them on this website as there is fierce competition on third party graded coins. The lowest priced coin will draw the most attention. But don't come here for wholesale pricing information because these dealers are pricing coins at retail to sell to collectors. Also be aware that although you can put coins in your cart, you cannot check out so that means that the coin can sell in a lot of other venues while you are waiting for the dealer to charge your card or take your check. Not too good for impulse buying!

The PCGS Coin Price Guide and the NGC Coin Price Values online websites were not much help either. Both offered stale retail prices, some were "staler" than others so they would be of little help to the novice dealer look for assistance. They just don't have a strong incentive to keep many thousands of prices fresh and up-to-date.

And lastly, we reviewed *Coin World* Coin Prices. Yes it is online; yes most U.S. coins are included. But it is left to the authors to determine which coins are best represented by prices in 10 grades or in 20 grades.

WHAT ABOUT THESE OTHER SOURCES OF PRICING?

Again they are retail prices and some are years old. But they are free with the magazine and free online with a print subscription.

For the dealer looking for prices as to what to pay for something, I would suggest a subscription to the *Greysheet* for the reasons listed when we covered it—widest array of pricing, prices are less than one month old and strong industry-wide support. The clear winner, in my estimation, is the *Greysheet*—"The Swiss Army Knife of the Coin Business."

(The April 2020 issue of the CDN Monthly Greysheet. Photo courtesy of Greysheet.)

04 | OTHER FACTORS AFFECTING PRICING

There are multiple factors that can increase or decrease the value of a certain coin. Some of these factors are: Strike, Luster, Provenance, and Toning. We will look at these characteristics separately.

STRIKE

Strike is the amount of detail on a coin after it is struck by the Mint. A coin can be weakly struck, have an average strike or it can be well-struck. While the amount of natural detail on a coin may not affect the grade of the coin in lower grades, it certainly does affect the grade of a coin in higher grades and it definitely does affect the price of a coin. However, NGC in their Coin Grading Scale state that an MS64 coin has to have "an average or better strike," and coins MS65 and higher require them to be "well struck." So strike is definitely important to the grading of Mint State coins.

MS/PF **69**	A fully struck coin with nearly imperceptible imperfections.
MS/PF **68**	Very sharply struck with only miniscule imperfections.
MS/PF **67**	Sharply struck with only a few imperfections.
MS/PF **66**	Very well struck with minimal marks and hairlines.
MS/PF **65**	Well struck with moderate marks and hairlines.
MS/PF **64**	Average or better strike with several obvious marks or hairlines and other miniscule imperfections.
MS/PF **63**	Slightly weak or average strike with moderate abrasions and hairlines of varying sizes.
MS/PF **62**	Slightly weak or average strike with no trace of wear. More or larger abrasions than an MS/PF 63.
MS/PF **61**	Weak or average strike with no trace of wear. More marks and/or multiple large abrasions.
MS/PF **60**	Weak or average strike with no trace of wear. Numerous abrasions, hairlines and/or large marks.

(NGC Coin Grading Scale – www.ngccoin.com/coin-grading/grading-scale/)

What can cause a weakly struck coin? There are two likely issues that can cause weak strikes—worn dies or uneven striking pressure. As the die strikes the metal coin blanks (planchets), the highest points of the design can start to wear down losing detail as it does. That means that the coin is now being struck from worn dies. That causes flat spots where detail once was.

Additionally, if both dies strike the coin simultaneously, the metal is pushed by the pressure to fill up the empty space (the high relief portions) in the dies. If one side has a great deal of space to fill in, it can cause the other die to not fill in properly. That uneven striking pressure can result in what is called an uneven strike.

Look at the pictures of the Draped Bust quarter below. The far left example is fully struck. The middle and far right examples are weakly struck, especially the details at the eagle's neck and head, the stars above the eagle's head and the top of the shield.

OTHER FACTORS AFFECTING PRICING

Fully Struck Example **Weakly Struck Example**

(Picture courtesy of PCGS – https://www.pcgs.com/news/difficult-to-grade-coins--part-four)

A weakly struck coin can significantly depress the price of a coin. Which of the coins above would you rather own? I think maybe 100% of people would pick the coin on the left. A strongly struck example will bring a premium over coins that are typically not well struck.

New Orleans "O" mint Morgan silver dollars, most Peace silver dollars, San Francisco "S" mint and Denver "D" mint Lincoln cents and Buffalo nickels from the 1910s to 1930s are typically not well-struck. So when you see a fully struck specimen of these coins it is unusual and likely a great coin to purchase.

Printed prices in the Greysheet and Red Book are for typical specimens, whether they typically are well-struck or not. So premiums for well-struck specimens can add as much as 50% to the value of a normally weakly struck coin.

But do NOT confuse a weakly struck coin with a worn (circulated) coin. The coin should display unbroken luster and no dull grey spots to be considered as an Uncirculated coin.

LUSTER

Luster is an important quality of a nice coin. So what is it and how did it get on my coin?

When a coin is struck, the softened metal flows into all of the design recesses that are in the die. This creates the relief on the coin and makes the details in the die visible. Letters, stars, Miss Liberty and all designs now appear as the die gets filled. As the metal

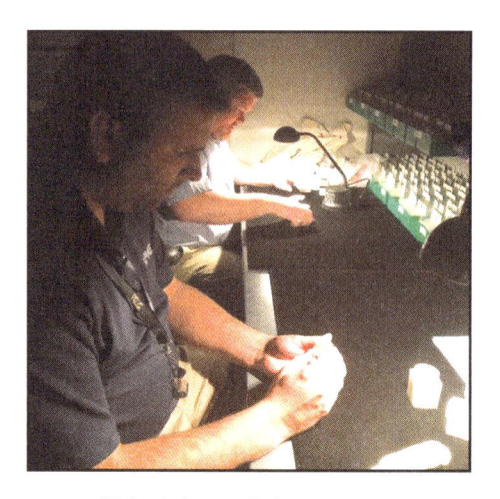

(Coins being graded at APMEX – Photo courtesy of APMEX.)

flows into the die, it generally slows in straight outward lines towards the edges of the die. The straight outward lines are called "radial flow lines." They are microscopic in size but they perform a very important function in grading a coin. To properly grade a coin, it is suggested that you hold the coin under a good incandescent light at a 45 degree angle in a darkened room.

Never try to grade coins using a florescent light—it distorts the luster of the coin and may hide hairlines or scratches. When you hold the coin under the light and slowly rotate the coin, the coin reflects light off of the radial flow lines back to your eyes. This produces what is commonly called "a cartwheel effect." That light being reflected back to you is what we call luster!

(The BRIGHT areas on both sides of this Barber half dollar are reflecting LUSTER back into your eyes. Photo courtesy of PCGS.)

When a die is highly polished and brand new, it may not reflect the light back into your eyes. Instead it may produce a "proof-like" surface which appears to be mirrored. With each subsequent coin that is struck, the "proof-like" surface diminishes a bit until it is completely gone and you begin to see luster instead of the mirrored surface. Coins with prooflike surfaces are eagerly sought by some collectors.

(A Prooflike Morgan Silver Dollar. Note the devices are frosted and the fields appear mirrored. Photo Courtesy of PCGS.)

As you can see, luster is an important characteristic of coins and the absence of any luster usually indicates a lower grade (or circulated) coin. Luster can be (from highest to lowest)—Booming, Average, or Satiny.

PROVENANCE

The provenance of a coin details the history of the ownership of that particular coin. It is a chronology of the previous owners of that exact coin. So why is this important and why does it affect the value of a coin?

For ancient coins the provenance is extremely important since there are relatively new cultural protection laws that prohibit the exporting of a country's historical artifacts. Some European and Middle Eastern nations have implemented Cultural Assets Protection laws that prohibit artifacts such as coins from being exported out of the country. The provenance may prove that the coin was here, in the United States, or at least out of the country of origin, decades or centuries before exporting them was problematic or illegal.

For United States coins, knowing a coin's provenance is important. Most collectors want to own a coin that was part of an important collection. With the advent of online sales and bidding two decades ago, it is easy to identify certain coins as coming from a particular collection and having been owned by important dealers or collectors. Sometimes prior auction tags or holders accompany the coin to assure that the provenance is real. While that is not actual proof (the coins may have been switched for another lesser quality coin), it is very helpful.

Additionally, the coin may have been a "plate" coin in an early reference book or early auction catalog. So having a coin's provenance can add significant value to the coin.

Some of the most famous U.S. coin collections are:

- Virgil Brand Collection
- The Stickney Collection
- The Parmalee Collection
- Ed Milas Collection
- T. Harrison Garrett Collection
- James Stack Collection
- Louis Eliasberg Collection
- The Clapp Collections
- The Norweb Collection
- Byron Reed Collection
- John Jay Pittman's Collection
- The King Farouk of Egypt Collection
- Harry Bass Collection
- Eric P. Newman Collection
- Mack & Brent Pogue Collection

These are just some of the more recent or prominent collections of United States coins. Auctions of any of the coins, or partial sets, from the above or other famous collections, positively creates news in the numismatic world.

(This magnificent Gold Brasher Doubloon, pedigreed to the Virgil Brand Collection realized $4.582 million at a Heritage Auctions sale in 2014. Photo courtesy of Heritage Auctions.)

So if you purchase a coin with an important provenance, it is important to keep the provenance associated with your particular coin(s). It can significantly increase the value of the coin for years to come. Inexpensive or common coins, even from important collections or hoards, do not generate significant additional dollars.

TONING

On silver coins, toning is a completely natural reaction to light, air and the environment (storage place) where a silver coin was stored. Generally speaking, the longer a coin is stored in that environment, the deeper the coin will tone. Silver is a chemically-active metal. Copper, nickel and to a lesser extent, gold coins may acquire color toning which first may start off very light, then move into pastel shades, then more vibrant colors, and finally very dark, and possibly, unattractive colors.

The layer of color is imparted on to the top surface layer of the coin. It, seemingly, protects the surfaces underneath. But the longer a coin is exposed to the environment which is toning the coin, the richer and then darker the color becomes. So "catching" the toning at the exact correct moment or peak toning is nearly impossible and in the eyes of the buyer. Some people love pastel toning on coins. Some people want rainbow toning, encompassing all of the primary colors of the rainbow in a pleasing manner. Appreciation of toning is ALWAYS subjective. Some dealers and collectors do not like toning, as it hides some of the coin's natural luster. So why would something that happens naturally (toning) bring multiples of what a coin, without toning would bring? That depends on how much YOU like that color.

On April 3, 2004, an auction company, Superior Galleries, held an auction in Santa Clara, California. The sale was called the "Santa Clara Elite Coin Auction."

Included in the sale was a beautiful coin—a 1926 Oregon Trail Commemorative Half Dollar. The coin was graded as MS67 and was worth somewhere near $2,000 in that grade.

But the coin did not fetch $2,000. It brought more. The lot, #1787, opened at $5,000—two and one half times the wholesale dealer Bid price for the coin. It proceeded to go up in price through $20,000. There were a half dozen bidders when the coin reached the $30,000 plateau—15 times the Greysheet price!

At the $40,000 level, 5 bidders remained and they continued to fight amongst each other to own this amazing coin. But going through to $50,000, three bidders had fallen by the wayside.

Now at $50,000—25 times the normal Bid price—there were two remaining bidders only. In $1,000 increments, the coin broke through the $60,000 level—30 times the Greysheet Bid price! The two bidders—both coin dealers—continued to bid the coin to higher and higher levels.

Finally at the incredible price of $69,000, one bidder stood alone. The coin had been purchased for 34.5 times the Greysheet bid of $2,000. Why did the coin bring so much money? Why did knowledgeable dealers fight over paying many multiples of what the coin was supposedly worth? What drove seemingly rational people to possibly overpay by tens of thousands of dollars?

"Beauty is in the eye of the beholder," is a famous quote by author Margaret Wolfe Hungerford, from her 1878 book, <u>Molly Brown</u>.

Was this coin the most beautiful 1926 Oregon Trail Commemorative Half Dollar that ever existed? And even if it was, was it worth 34.5 times bid?

You be the judge...

The coin is as beautiful today as it was in 2004 when it appeared in the auction. The coin has been resubmitted for grading review to PCGS and no longer is graded MS67. It now resides in a PCGS MS68+ holder and is the finest known. There are three coins graded MS68 but this is the only coin that grades as MS68+ and there are no coins graded higher.

Spectacular, does not do the coin justice. But the lofty price paid 16 years ago assures that this is the "Finest Known" specimen. Does that mean there will never be another MS68+ or a MS69? No!

OTHER FACTORS AFFECTING PRICING

(The 1926 Oregon Trail Commemorative Half Dollar that was purchased for $69,000 – Photo courtesy of PCGS Coinfacts – https://www.pcgs.com/coinfacts/coin/1926-50c-oregon/9340)

With an original mintage of 47,955, anything is possible. But given that approximately 35 years have passed since the two major grading services began accepting submissions, the likelihood of a superior example existing in a collection somewhere diminishes day-by-day.

Did the dealers overpay for this coin? Did the current collector, who owns this coin, overpay for it? History will be the judge on that day when this amazing coin comes back to the auction block. But the current owner has, arguably, the finest Classic Commemorative collection currently known to man, so it just isn't available—perhaps no matter how much money you have!

Only one coin can be the finest and, for a 1926 Oregon Trail commemorative half dollar—this is it!

To paraphrase Margaret Wolfe Hungerford,

Beauty is in the eye of the Buyer!

05 | THE IMPACT OF ONLINE MARKETPLACES AND CERTIFIED COINS

The Numismatic world never remains static. What was popular yesterday may not be so popular tomorrow. That includes both products and sources of information.

Online information is technologically evolving at a rapid pace. The CDN Exchange and CCE battle each other to offer dealers across the country better and faster communications, impressive options and ease of creating Bid and Ask prices for certified coins.

NUMISMATIC TECHNOLOGICAL HISTORY

In the 1960s, the dominant technology in the numismatic world was the teletype system. A service called the Fox and Crabbe Teletype System (FACTS) was the dominant player and a number of larger coin dealers had a noisy and large teletype machine eating "green

(An old Teletype machine used on the FACTS coin network. Photo courtesy of Collectors Universe.)

bar" daisy wheel printer paper by the boxful. Dealers posted messages to buy and sell all kinds of coins but brilliant uncirculated rolls of modern coins were the darlings of the day.

In the 1980s, (February, 1986), the Professional Coin Grading Service (PCGS) was founded in Irvine, CA. PCGS began authenticating, grading and encapsulating coins. The move was innovative in several respects. PCGS sought to establish a standard for grading coins and all coins were required to meet those standards. Additionally, they would grade coins by consensus, where multiple expert graders would have to agree on the grade of a coin before the grade would be assigned. Further, PCGS established a network of dealer-members who would bid on PCGS-graded coins on a sight-unseen basis. That fact that the network would make bids on coins without first seeing them was revolutionary.

Although the American Numismatic Association Certification Service (ANACS) had been authenticating and grading coins as an independent third party for years before PCGS ever existed, they never encapsulated their coins. They took black and white photos of them instead. And, more importantly, they did not have an active dealer network that would make offers to bid on ANACS-graded coins on a sight-unseen basis.

That network gave PCGS numismatic coins liquidity nearly rival-

(A PCGS First-Generation holder with coin – 'A Rattler' – Courtesy of PCGS.)

ing that of stocks and bonds. This electronic network that was established was called ANIE (American Numismatic Information Exchange) and 100 well-capitalized dealer-members could place bids on any of the nearly 200,000 coins listed on ANIE. This not only improved liquidity on numismatic coins, but it also helped to standardize pricing of PCGS graded coins.

(An NGC First Generation coin holder and coin – very much in demand today. Courtesy of CoinWeek.)

About a year later, another group of dealers created the Numismatic Guaranty Corporation (NGC)(then, of Parsippany, NJ), which would rival PCGS. NGC also authenticated, graded and encapsulated coins. They also graded coins by consensus and established their own grading standards. Each company sought to outdo the other with special pricing, additional services and better and more secure holders in which the coins were encapsulated. NGC rivaled PCGS, like Ford rivaled Chevy. But competition was good for the market, good for dealers and good for collectors.

The ANIE online trading system was replaced in 1990 by the Certified Coin Exchange (CCE) which absorbed all of the previously-existing ANIE dealers and bidders. In 2005, CCE was purchased by Collectors Universe, the parent company of PCGS.

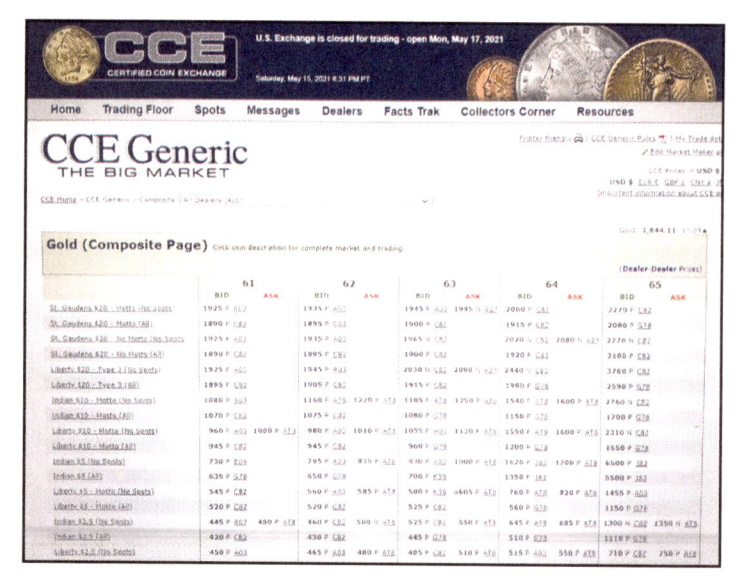

(A home page for the Certified Coin Exchange CCE – Courtesy of CCE.)

Around 2011, Coinplex was created to offer another option to dealers wishing to trade certified coins online. Coinplex competed with CCE openly. But Coinplex was a target of the Coin Dealer Newsletter (CDN).

A FORCE IN PRINT AND ONLINE

The Greysheet started in 1963 as a weekly pricing publication subscription sold to coin dealers. The Greysheet took its pricing from published coin buying lists, the four teletype systems, dealers' trades and auction prices realized.

But this weekly publication was inadequate as the market gained steam and prices changed much more rapidly and many more products and series came into the mainstream of dealers' shops. In 1976, CDN added a Monthly Summary, expanding on many of the most popular series and instead of using a generic "type" price, it now reported specific prices for all dates and mintmarks in a variety of grades.

The 1980s brought two additional innovations to the CDN. In 1980, the first Greensheet for currency was published on a monthly basis and it is still published today. Additionally, in 1986 as PCGS came into play, the CDN created a Bluesheet for PCGS and NGC graded coinage.

In 1992 the CDN added three new Quarterly issues which expanded coverage in both Uncirculated and Proof of many different type coins. The next change came in 2015 when the Downing family sold the Greysheet to a new management team but the publications and innovations continued.

The Coinplex system was purchased by CDN in 2015 and renamed the CDN Exchange. The CDN Exchange has rapidly improved to the point where it is today with a very fast-growing group of dealers, over $1 billion in bids, a dealer to dealer network and messaging system and numerous other features.

By 2018, CDN combined its weekly, monthly and quarterly pricing information into one monthly print and online publication which now included modern Chinese coin issues as well. Also in 2018, CDN published quarterly the CPG® Coin and Currency Market review, which provided retail values for U.S. coins. In 2019, CDN provided yet another new publication, the CAC Rare Coin Market Review, establishing printed prices for certified coins that have been approved by the Certified Acceptance Corporation (CAC).

(A typical Greysheet Publication – Courtesy of Coin Dealer Newsletter.)

Since 1963, the CDN family of publications and online offerings have become the backbone of the coin industry and the dealer lexicon of "What's Greysheet Bid?" has been forever impacted.

CERTIFIED COINS IN DEMAND

As demand for certified coins increased, the grading services continued to make it harder and harder for those people selling coins that were counterfeit or doctored—meaning something had been done to them to improve their appearance. An enterprising coin "doctor" would add toning to a coin to hide hairlines, scratches, or other imperfections. Both NGC and PCGS had expert graders who could detect such shenanigans done to coins to "improve" them.

Demand from collectors for certified coins began to increase. Some older collectors bemoaned the fact that they couldn't actually touch their coins any longer or place them in albums as they had been doing for decades. Some older dealers refused to "pay someone to grade their coins."

But for the most part, when a dealer sold a coin that wasn't certified—a "raw" coin—at a specific price commensurate with that stated grade, he now might find a collector coming back to him after a few months with those once raw coins now sitting in PCGS or NGC slabs and having to explain the differences in grades between what he thought and what NGC or PCGS thought. The dealers who sold—knowingly or unknowingly—over-graded or doctored coins now had to explain to their customers that either they (the dealers) were duped, couldn't grade or they didn't care. This truly caused a shift in the marketplace. Dealers needed to improve their grading standards and fast because their customers demanded more and more independently-graded coins.

A story here—in 1987 I went to the American Numismatic Association's annual coin show held in Cincinnati that year. I was sharing my dealer table with a dealer friend of mine. He had two cases full of PCGS coins and a smattering of brand new NGC coins. My inventory at the time consisted of one case of PCGS coins and a case of raw coins and a few miscellaneous boxes of coins. As we both were setting our inventories into showcases, an older dealer leaned over the table and after looking at our inventories stood there shaking his head. He looked at me and then at the coins and said, "A year from now you will have cracked your coins out of all of that plastic and you will be crying to me that you spent so much money on having someone tell you what grade your coins are." I tried to be nice to the gentleman who couldn't possibly understand why a dealer would pay to have his coins graded. All I could say in response was "you might be right." But I knew he was wrong. As much as he and a few others resisted this "innovation" I knew it was here to stay. It leveled the playing field for collectors and investors who prior to certification had to rely upon the knowledge, honesty and integrity of the coin dealer who sold them coins.

The impact that certified coins has had on the coin market is immeasurable. But as coins became traded like commodities, the volatility in the coin market also soared. Coins could climb very rapidly in price which pleased buyers and sellers alike. In the "HOT" coin market of 1985–1989 lots of dealers made lots of money even when they paid 20% over Bid for a coin. Why? Because next week the new Bid would be 20% higher and you could sell last week's coin at break-even money but no one did that. The following week the coin would be higher still.

During that period of 1985 through June of 1989, the rare coin market was on FIRE! Prices were running higher and higher. Wall Street investment firms, now that rare coins were a commodity, were dipping their toes in the water. Everyone was making money faster and faster.

Coins were bringing record prices at auction and on bourse floors across the country. It was really an amazing time to be a coin dealer. You couldn't help but make money. Most every series was in demand and brought prices that would have been unthinkable just 10 years earlier. Much of the momentum and demand was because of certified coins. But was the market really that hot?

Think I am kidding?

Will that ever happen again? Will prices ever approach those lofty levels? It seems unlikely. But, nothing is impossible. I stayed on the path of going to coin shows and buying and selling coins at shows. Most dealers did. But not all.

This dealer took a different path. A long-time friend of mine is Massachusetts dealer Andy Seminerio. Andy owns Victorian Rare Coins. I met Andy at coin shows across New England. Whatever show

SECRETS OF THE RARE COIN AND BULLION BUSINESS

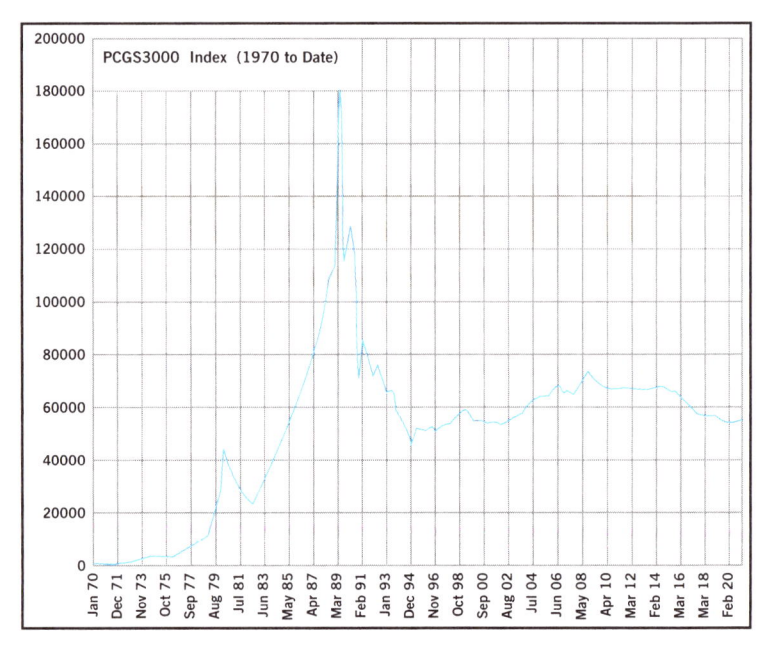

(This is a graph of the PCGS 3000 Rare Coin Index. Look at the trajectory of prices in 1985 to 1989. Courtesy of PCGS.)

I attended no matter how small, how large, or how far away it was—Andy was there. We competed for the same coins from other dealers and bought and sold coins to each other. From 1979 when I started full-time in the business until about 1987, Andy was everywhere.

The market was still going up when he stopped going to coin shows! Why would he do that? Andy found a different way of buying and selling coins. Andy decided that traveling to coin shows all across the country was not what he wanted to do.

As ANIE became a reality in 1987, Andy started to trade his certified coins online. His philosophy was, why do I need to go to a show, spend the money for plane fare, hotels, bourse tables, food and supplies? Why do I need to take the risk of traveling with my valuable inventory across the country and risk getting robbed, or take risks at all? Why not stay in my office and put my entire inventory online and look for coins that are attractively priced that I can buy online? It was a life changing decision for Andy.

The benefit was no traveling, none of the risks associated with traveling, more time with his family and a more regimented lifestyle. The downside was, of course, by not attending coin shows, he found out the latest news a bit later than those of us who were at the shows. But from his vantage point in his office he could study which dealers were bidding aggressively, and who wasn't. He also could see dealers putting up new bids quickly or taking them down quickly and he could trade on that news.

The path that Andy took wasn't the traditional path but it certainly has worked for him. Most dealers work their online activity as a part of what they do, in addition to attending shows, going to auctions, etc. But Andy has made a great impact on the coin market simply by staying in his office.

Today Andy is one of the major "Market Makers" on CCE, with thousands of Bids and Asks and millions of dollars of exposure in the rare coin market. New dealers today have no idea who Andy is unless they trade with him on CCE. The point is, the market is always changing and your niche may not be the traditional one. Andy kept his eyes open, embraced the new technology of the day, and evolved with it.

COLLECTORS CORNER – IS ACTUALLY FOR DEALERS

Collectors Corner (www.CollectorsCorner.com) is an online marketplace where dealers who are members of CCE can list their coins on one large website. It is owned by Collectors Universe, the parent company of PCGS. The website boasts of having over 169,000 coins, representing nearly $320 million from 125 active dealers.

Unlike eBay or most other coin websites, you cannot actually BUY coins on Collectors Corner. When you see a coin that you like, the price is right and you want it, you can drop it in your shopping cart and Collectors Corner notifies the advertising dealer and either the buyer contacts the dealer or, more likely, the dealer contacts you. You then buy the coin direct from the dealer. This website gives PCGS/CCE dealers another venue to sell their coins, but to a collector audience.

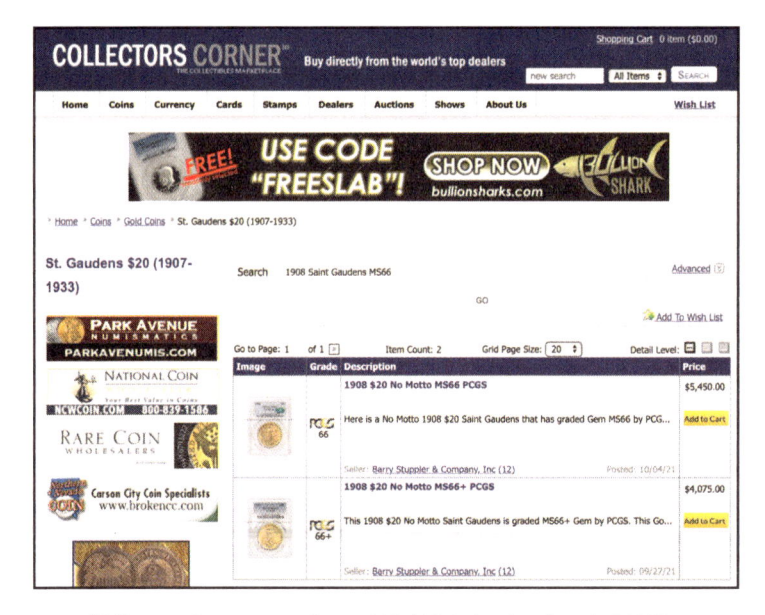

(Collectors Corner page for a 1908 $20 Saint-Gaudens in MS66 – Courtesy of www.CollectorsCorner.com)

Collector Corner will also allow the dealers to list currency, stamps and cards (sports and non-sports) that have been certified. The major auction houses that are members of CCE will also list the lots in their upcoming auctions so you may bid on them from this website as well.

COINWORLD MARKETPLACE

The venerable CoinWorld newspaper that so many of us grew up reading has also developed an online trading marketplace for coins. The site allows dealers to trade in their one-stop convenient marketplace.

Their website (www.CoinWorld.market) has a couple of dozen dealers and more than 50,000 coins available for sale, valued at over $55 million.

A major difference in why collectors go to the CoinWorld marketplace is that unlike Collectors Corner, you can actually buy coins on their website. As an innovation, they offer an escrow checkout which allows you to purchase a coin, send the payment online directly to CoinWorld where it is placed in escrow and released to the dealer when the coin is delivered.

This allows for a seamless transaction and unlike eBay, the dealers are all well-known in the industry and well-capitalized.

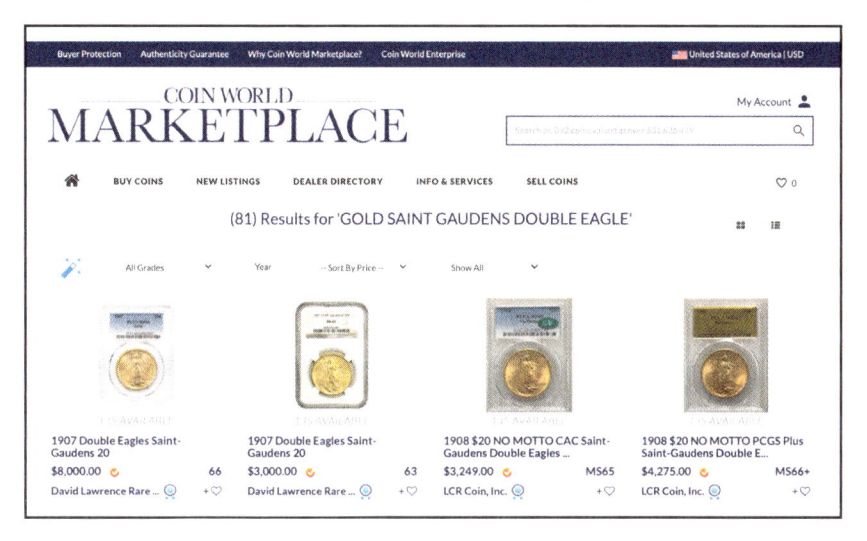

(A screenshot from the CoinWorld Marketplace – Photo courtesy of CoinWorld Marketplace.)

FACEBOOK GROUPS (THE WILD WEST)

One venue that MUST be discussed is the playground of dealers, collectors, investors and probable charlatans alike—and that is the hundreds, if not thousands, of coin groups on FaceBook!

Log onto your FaceBook account, go to Groups and type in "Coin Groups" and literally thousands of groups about coins or having the word "Coins" in their name appear. You can search for Public or Private groups.

As a dealer, I have been to more than 100 groups. Some are great, honest and reliable with thousands of members. Some are "fronts" for unscrupulous people to sell coins or bullion that may be of spurious origin. I have seen counterfeit coins, artificially toned coins, and wonderful amazing and expensive original coins all being sold on FaceBook.

How do you tell a good group from a not-so-good one? Well look at the number of members it has, look at how long it's been around, look at the rules that it asks members to abide by and look at what payment types are accepted for trading. You always want to have some recourse if the seller on the other send of your transaction decides not to send you the ½ Ounce Gold Krugerrand that you just purchased. What should you look for to help you determine is a FaceBook group is reliable?

- How many members does it have?
- Are there questions or requirements to join?
- How long has it been around?
- How active is it?
- Is it for information only? Or can you buy and sell?
- What are the rules for Buying and Selling?
- Are there a sufficient number of Administrators/Moderators in the group?
- How many messages are posted daily in the group?
- Are there dealers who have websites or are well-known in the group?
- Can you ask questions and get quick and reasonable answers to them from the Mods?
- What types of payment are acceptable?

Use your common sense. If prices in a particular group seem too good to be true, something is wrong. If very few people are selling or trading anything at all, be wary.

Now that I have scared you, I will also tell you that you can buy decent products (coins or bullion) at lower prices here more often than you can find from dealers or on eBay.

But if you are not very knowledgeable in authentication, grading and pricing, there is always some level of risk. Join a group or three, watch the posts, get comfortable with how it works, talk to some sellers or buyers, but do not spend any money until you have a good idea of how the group seems to you. Be careful—but have fun. Those two things are NOT mutually exclusive.

THE IMPACT OF ONLINE MARKETPLACES AND CERTIFIED COINS

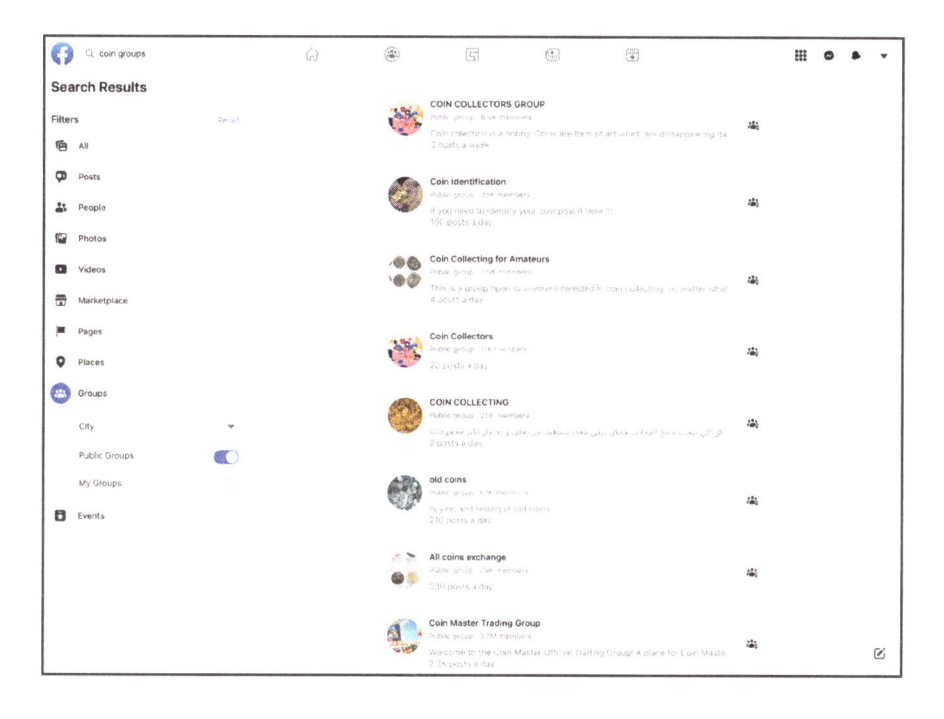

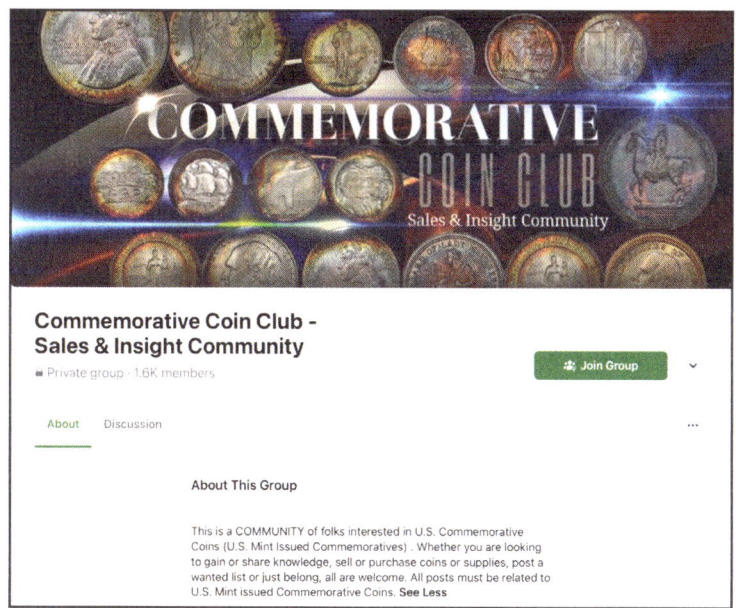

(Top – A search for Public Coin Groups. Bottom – A private Commemorative Coin Group – Courtesy of FaceBook.)

06 | THOUSANDS OF ONLINE SELLERS

As I write this chapter, the Coronavirus is surging in 26 states. Shows like Long Beach, Baltimore, Central States, have all been canceled. The few coin shows that have gone forward did so in a manner much different than what we have been use to at any point in our lives. Limited dealers in any room, one customer per dealer, masks, social distancing are all the new normal now. Even the granddaddy of them all—the ANA's annual World's Fair of Money was canceled. That does not take into account the countless smaller regional and local shows that have all been canceled. This is the fact of life for coin dealers so how can you sell coins in this brave new world?

If you are a novice dealer and want to sell lots and lots of coins today, simply go online! That is how easy people make it sound. But it isn't that easy and you have LOTS and LOTS of decisions to make. You can build your own website (the hardest way) or have someone build it for you (the most expensive way) or simply join a selling platform such as FaceBook or eBay (the easiest way). So what are the benefits and drawbacks of each?

THE DO-IT-YOURSELFER

Building a website today is pretty easy. Companies like GoDaddy (www.GoDaddy.com) give you all the tools to build a functioning website by taking their templates and adjusting the text and uploading pictures. The amount of programming knowledge required borders on ZERO!

You can load multiple pages, start a blog; it is really simple to do many things today as the templates are created for you. They have step-by-step guides but most of them are fairly intuitive. That's the good part!

The bad part is that, to paraphrase a popular movie line, "If you build it, will they come?" You still need to be recognized by the web crawlers that determine which websites rank higher than others. The algorithms were previously based on the numbers of times certain key words were used. Ah, those were the days!

It is no longer like that. Now, in order to rank higher you need web content that makes sense. You need content that allows them to determine that you have more information about the item in the web search than anyone else. So between buying inventory, prepping it for sale, placing the items on the website, taking photographs and now writing unique content about them—it is a full-time job—for multiple people.

But that kind of content draws people to your website and to the products that you are selling. Years ago, you never talked about or shared your secret knowledge with anyone. Anyone! That information was YOUR big advantage. Today if you don't give that info away, you don't rank highly.

When I worked for APMEX, I held executive positions and did executive tasks. Today, since I retired from APMEX, I actively write content for them. Why? The best copywriters in the world are not quite as good as people who can write reasonably well but, more importantly, have spent 20, 30, 40 years perfecting their crafts. They know the jargon and when to use it, they know how to make people understand what they already know and they know how their (your) market really does work. There is no learning curve with them—they already get it!

The D-I-Y method gives you complete control and you can change or adapt anything at YOUR convenience. But there is a level of sophistication that is hard to attain when you do it all yourself. The fact is—you might never get there at all!

THE ROYAL TREATMENT

Finding a do-it-yourself website builder is cheaper but some choices of available templates are limited and some are not. You might not find what you are looking for your business. Most website templates really aren't for coin dealers or sellers.

But a professional web designer knows the current market trends and knows what you might need even better that YOU do. They know what was "last year's chic" and what people want to see in a modern website built for today.

These website companies can take your vision and run with it making it better, faster and more efficient for doing business than you ever dreamed. And they understand the user experience far better than the average layman.

Web developers can build a website for you that attracts web crawlers and attracts customers—it is exactly what they do! They understand it. If their website attracted you to their business, there is probably a good reason for it. They know what they are doing.

And they can deliver a better product than you can build and likely faster too. But this all comes at a price. In fact, every time you want to upload an image or add some text or change something that they have coded into your website you hear—ca-ching! They are billing you.

That's really the downside. If your website goes down at 2AM, can you call them? Is someone on duty? You can get that 24/7 assurance—for a price.

The biggest issue is that if you do it yourself you can use the right text and know which images strike a responsive chord for the message that you are trying to convey. Teaching that to someone else who doesn't know you, your beliefs, your industry, is hard and time consuming.

But having a professional do it for you eliminates a lot of trial and error issues and gets you looking more professional much faster. Everything is a tradeoff—one way or another.

To save money a number of coin dealers have engaged off-shore programmers due to their exceptionally low cost. But is that a risk worth taking? You have multiple time zones to work through when you need corrective action FAST! Is there a language barrier? What if your website crashes at an odd time for them? Can they restore your service quickly? I am not convinced.

One other consideration—what happens to your website when you decide that the virus is no longer a threat to you? What happens when all of the shows start up again and are in full swing? Do you stay at home, miss the shows, and update your website? Do you stop paying someone to host your website? If it goes down while you were at a show, who will notice (besides your customers), who will update it? Who will maintain it. If you are an active dealer do you continue to update your website while you are buying and selling at the shows? Is all of this worth it?

THE BIG ENCHILADA – THE EBAY PLATFORM

You can easily skip all of the build your own website headaches simply. You can set up your business on eBay or Amazon or any other platform that has members who will see your storefront or web page. Depending on their customer base and how large it is, you may have dozens to thousands of people looking at your offerings. Let's talk about eBay.

The usual process is the platform takes a listing fee and a final value fee (probably about 10–20%—eBay is at 11 %!). eBay requires you to use PayPal to settle your sales (at another 3%)! Can you give up 14% of your SALES PROCEEDS—NOT YOUR MARGIN and still make a living? Is it worth it to sell on their platform if it costs that much? If you are a wholesaler making 10-15% on your quick flips—can you afford to give most of that up so you don't have to build and maintain your own website?

I can give you 174,000,000 reasons why you should still sell on eBay! That is the number of "Active eBay Marketplace buyers worldwide" according to eBay.

Q1 FAST FACTS

174M	$21.3B	$2.4B	65%
Active eBay Marketplace buyers worldwide	Amount of eBay Marketplace GMV	eBay Inc. reported revenue	International eBay Inc. revenue

https://investors.ebayinc.com/overview/default.aspx – courtesy of eBayinc.com

The eBay platform reaches probably 1 out of every 3 Americans. Everyone has heard or seen their commercials on radio, TV and especially on the web. eBay "Ya, we've got that!" was a very familiar tagline. **Your** customers will see **you** on eBay.

One slight problem for you, Mr. Dealer, is that they will see the thousands and thousands of other dealers on eBay too! In Chapter Two (the Pricing Chapter) we went looking for an 1881-CC Morgan Silver Dollar in MS66 graded by PCGS on eBay and—we found 23 of them. And the price varied between $1,175 and $1,965 for the EXACT same coin! So there is an advantage for buyers in that there is competition.

But if you sell on eBay, you have good, competitive prices, great customer service, and your own website, you may be able to tempt buyers to buying directly off of your website. How? eBay doesn't make it easy. Exchanging phone numbers or email addresses is reason to kick you off of eBay. How do dealers capture customers off of eBay?

It's simple! Offer great coins at highly competitive prices, write up accurate and knowledgeable descriptions, teach your customers what they need to know and as you deliver products that you sold on eBay, include your business card and some type of offer such as 10% off your first purchase on our website. That may get your customer to visit your website. They already have confidence in you and that will grow based on how much business you can do.

But remember, you have to maintain it and update it and offer items cheaper than on eBay. But the sales price is YOURS—you aren't sharing it with eBay or any other selling platform. You will have your website expenses of course but that should be a lot less than 14% per month. But you are signing up for a lot of work.

EBAY FOR BUYERS – IT'S SCARY OUT THERE!

As a buyer, eBay gives you lots and lots and lots and lots to choose from—maybe too much. There are many dealers and many items from which to choose. Obviously, you need to comparison shop. Do your research (Greysheet) and find a good price and see how close you can come.

But, Mr. Coin Buyer, how do you know what you're getting is a good deal? Are you certain the coin is genuine and original? If you don't like the coin, or it doesn't match the description or picture, what is your recourse? Some dealers charge a 10–20% restocking fee if you return it. On an expensive coin that can really add up!

Well, wait a minute! "I only buy PCGS or NGC 'slabbed' coins! In that way I know my coins are original and genuine." When buying a PCGS or NGC graded coin from a reliable dealer—that is true. From a dealer that you haven't heard of, with a low number of eBay feedback points, well that could be risky. How?

How do YOU know that the slab itself isn't counterfeit? A trustworthy dealer stakes his/her reputation on selling you genuine NGC or PCGS coins in the proper slabs. An unethical dealer on eBay can wreak havoc. Where would they get these coins? Who would make them? Wouldn't it be hard to do? Wouldn't it be a risky thing to do?

Risky—YES! Difficult—NO, unfortunately. I wandered over to a well-known website based in China and searched for Gold American Eagle 1 Ounce bullion coins. Here is one of many responses:

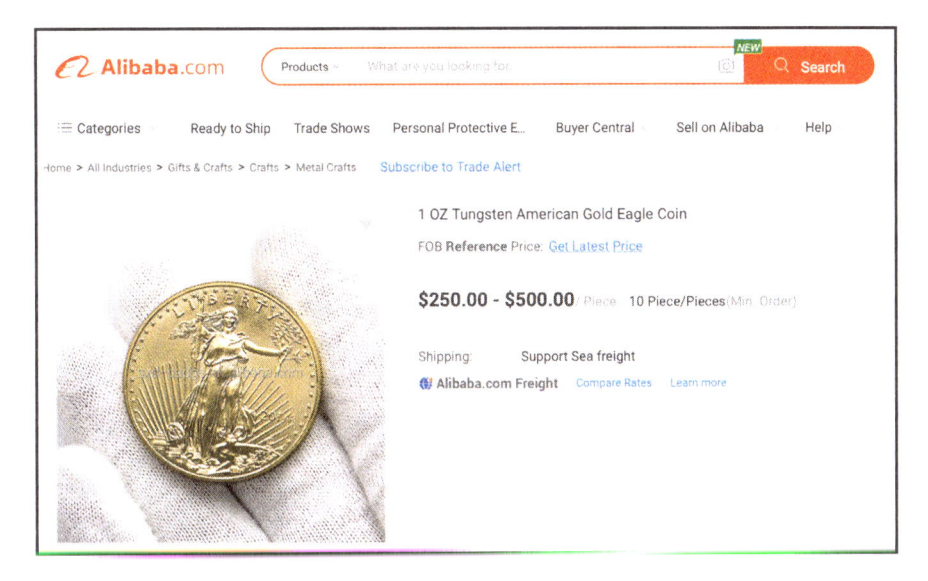

(A Fake Gold American Eagle advertised on a Chinese website. Photo courtesy of the Author.)

A genuine U.S. Mint product will cost you at the time this was written, with Gold at $1,815.00, between $1,900 and $2,000 each. The Chinese "Replica" is priced at $250 to $500 each, depending on the quantity that you order. Why is a REPLICA coin so expensive? First, the coin is not stamped with the word "REPLICA" or "COPY or "FACSIMILE" or any notation on it to indicate it is NOT the real thing.

Second, the underlying base metal is tungsten. Why use much more expensive tungsten rather than lead or brass? Well it is non-magnetic and most importantly, if you throw it on a scale it will weigh almost exactly like gold does. Third, it is gold—PLATED which means that it will have the appearance of gold.

To the untrained eye, it just might pass for the real thing! If you placed one of those coins in a PCGS or NGC holder, how would eBay know it isn't genuine and how would they know to kill that listing on their site? Well with almost 1.2 MILLION United States coins advertised, the answer is they wouldn't know! If you price it close to the average eBay price for one—it would be like finding a needle in a haystack!

SECRETS OF THE RARE COIN AND BULLION BUSINESS

But where could you get a PCGS-style holder in which to encapsulate it? Hmmmmmm...

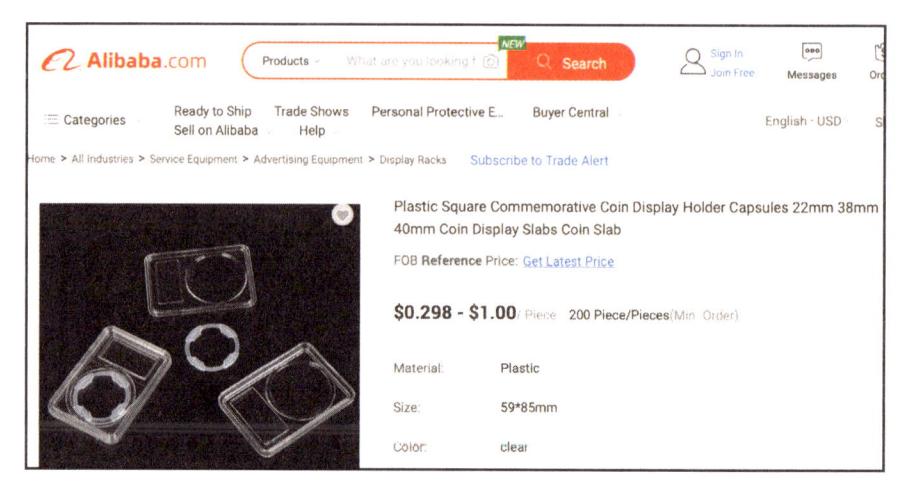

(A Fake PCGS-style holder available on that same Chinese website. Photo courtesy of the Author.)

Is it only PCGS-graded coins that you have to watch out for? No... Here is a fake NGC-style holder also from that infamous Chinese website.

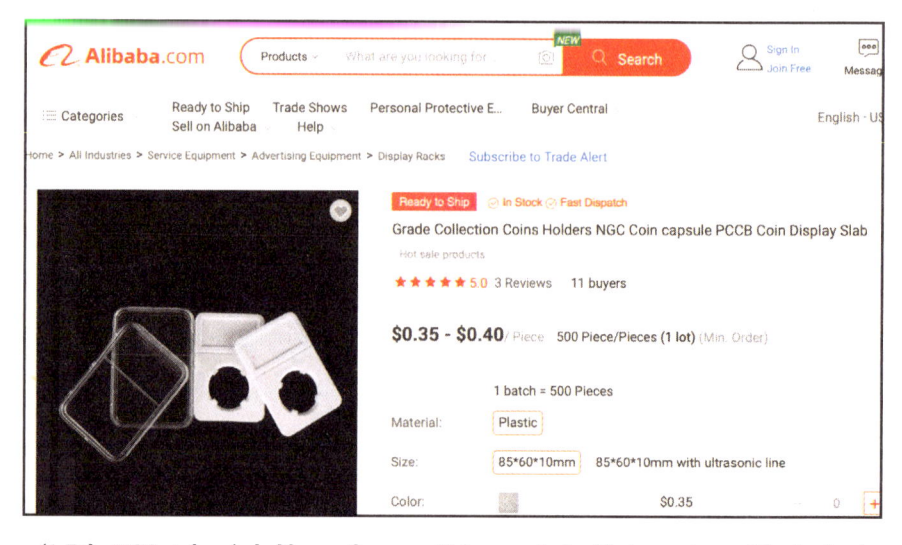

(A Fake NGC-style coin holder on the same Chinese website. Photo courtesy of the Author.)

Chinese counterfeits have plagued the coin hobby for decades and it isn't getting any better. In fact as technology advances, the counterfeiters get better and better at what they do and both PCGS and NGC are working very hard and spend millions of dollars trying to stay one step ahead of them. Remember, it is not illegal in China to "copy" a different coinage and make these replica coins. The ones that come in stamped as "COPY" or "REPLICA" pose little threat. These unstamped coins are another matter entirely.

So, how do you protect yourself from buying counterfeit products on eBay or Amazon or anywhere?

KNOW YOUR DEALER

Well the best rule is—know your dealer. Do they offer a great no questions asked return policy for at least 10–14 days after receipt? If they do, that is a great sign. Do they not charge you a restocking fee? Another positive sign.

Next—check their feedback. If they have tons of happy customers (when they are SELLERS) that is another great sign. Also check their memberships—American Numismatic Association (ANA), Professional Numismatists Guild (PNG), Professional Coin Grading Service member (PCGS), Numismatic Guaranty Corporation member (NGC), Certified Acceptance Corporation (CAC), CDN Exchange, or Certified Coin Exchange memberships—all of these are great indicators that the company is honest and most important legitimate. If your seller has lots of positive points, rest assured they should be reputable.

Another tool in your arsenal as an eBay buyer is to pay with PayPal. They have a reputation of generally siding with the BUYERS in most transactions. If the item isn't as described, you can return it for a full refund. Keep receipts and return using tracking numbers and you will be fine.

But the next time you see a coin that is priced more cheaply and the seller states "NO RETURNS" think long and hard about what you might possibly be getting into when they do not back up what they sell. Some sellers state: NO RETURNS ON CERTIFIED COINS! Given how many millions of coins that PCGS and NGC have graded there will certainly be a number of mistakes. It is unavoidable. So find a dealer with liberal return policies and give them a try. Many dealers are willing to stand behind their coins regardless of whether the coins you purchase are slabbed or raw so look for their terms of sale to understand how well you are being protected.

One more benefit if you sell on eBay is that eBay automatically charges the Buyer the appropriate amount of sales tax for their location and in accordance with their regulations. They collect and remit it to the appropriate state of residence for the buyer. This has made it easy for even small sellers to use eBay and not worry about the 1,700+ different taxing authorities (State, County, School District, etc.) who want you to collect and remit taxes to them. If eBay did not do this for their sellers, there would be much, fewer sellers on eBay and only the large companies would survive that scenario.

There are no fool-proof guarantees in life—other than death and taxes—but finding dealers who have nice coins at reasonable prices that are genuine and are coins that they stand behind is not difficult! But you must do your due diligence first!

THE "TWILIGHT ZONE" KNOWN AS FACEBOOK

If you log onto FaceBook and search "Groups" for "U.S. Coins" you will be amazed at the number of groups that display. Some groups are legitimate and have thousands of members. They are active, provide information and allow buying and selling.

Other groups are not so legitimate or have been abandoned by the original administrators. Some FaceBook groups are well managed. The Administrators and Moderators (who are all volunteers by the way), do a pretty good job of keeping the riff-raff out. And if a seller doesn't follow through or a buyer never pays for the lots that he has won, a good group will try to reach out to the parties and mediate a settlement. If all else fails, removing the offending party by banning

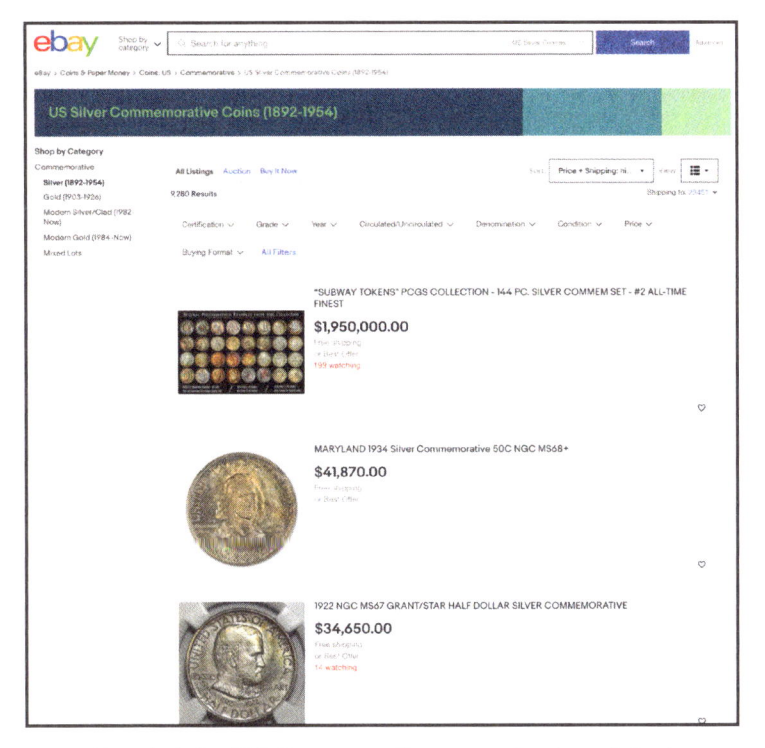

(A typical eBay U.S. Commemoratives page – Courtesy of eBay.)

them from the group stops it from happening again but if YOU paid for something and didn't receive it, you have little recourse. Be very careful in FaceBook groups, which is why I am making this statement.

The problem is each group's and every member's situations are fluid and can change minute by minute. Someone who paid well and quickly last week may have run out of money and be "needy" now. Unlike eBay where you post a credit card for charges against your PayPal account, FaceBook has no such rules.

FaceBook sellers usually accept a wide variety of payment plans. The typical means of paying for winnings on FaceBook include: PayPal, Venmo, eCheck, Money Orders, Checks, Zelle, CashApp, and FB Messenger Pay and others. Each of these has their own fees, and safety precautions. As you check them out, make sure that each of them can protect you—the buyer. Some protections are better than others and some of these offer little or no protection and it all comes down to cost. PayPal is one of the most costly but when your hard-earned money is at risk, you want all of the protection that you can get.

Since there is no feedback system on FaceBook, how do you tell a good seller from a bad one? That is a hard question to answer. But here is the BEST THING that you can do: ASK FOR REFERENCES. And then actually check them out. In the Group where the sale is taking place is a great place to start.

A typical message for references would be: "Looking to do business with Fred Smith of ABC Coin Company in Oklahoma City? Who knows him and has recently done business with him as a seller? Reply on open or via DM (direct message). Thanks!"

If no one steps up to vouch for your seller, think again about whether dealing with him is worth the risk. Maybe, ask for PayPal immediate payment. FaceBook, unlike PayPal and eBay, was set up to be social media. This developed later into a marketplace so it doesn't have the safeguards built in like eBay does. But FB is not charging you a fee like eBay does.

There are lots and lots of decisions to make as a dealer and each one will cost you money and ultimately decide how successful you will be. Every platform is different, charges different rates and has different benefits. And building your website can also become costly and it is a time-consuming project. Whatever you decide, throw yourself fully into it. Don't do a project unless you can put your best foot forward. Remember, you only have one opportunity to make that first impression with your customers. Don't blow it!

07 | ALL ABOUT APMEX – A DIFFERENT KIND OF ONLINE SELLER

For the sake of transparency to you, dear reader, I am going to tell you about APMEX, and also tell you that I once worked there. I spent 11 years at that company and I want to give you an insider's view of what APMEX is like, what it is like to work there, and how it grew so quickly and why APMEX is a company that I highly recommend for many different reasons.

In 2008, I had been in the coin business as a full-time dealer for about 30 years. I had operated my own business, Liberty Numismatics, and was primarily a wholesale dealer. Later, after gathering a sufficient number of collectors and investors who placed their trust in me, I operated as a retail coin dealer. In the interim, I was also the Director of Wholesale for a very large retail coin dealer.

My experience with APMEX literally changed my life. I had lived in New England for 55 years. We were settled there, my daughter was a freshman at a college in Boston. And the coin and bullion markets were heating up. I had NO intention of giving up my business and moving 1,500 miles south!

At that time, Scott Thomas, the President and Founder of APMEX, was really just starting to grow his bullion business. Scott hadn't planned on building a coin and bullion business. So how did he get started?

IN THE BEGINNING...

Scott's grandfather operated a small mail order coin business. When Scott was a boy he loved to spend time with his grandfather who would have Scott search through rolls of pennies and nickels looking for those dates that Scott needed to fill his blue Whitman coin folders. Scott was bitten by "the bug"—he loved the thrill of the hunt, as do all collectors. Finding the right coin to add to your collection, whether it is upgrading existing coins or filling an elusive open hole in the album is a thrill to a real collector.

In 1982, Scott's grandfather passed away and the family decided to leave his inventory intact and deal with it at another time. But in 1999, the family home in New York needed to be sold so his grandfather's inventory became Scott's responsibility to liquidate. Scott first offered these collector coins at a local antique market in Oklahoma and then on eBay. He was surprisingly successful at selling these coins given the market conditions at the time.

In early 2000, Scott had opened up a small coin shop in a strip mall in Edmond, Oklahoma and called it Edmond Coins. Not only was he selling coins from his grandfather's collection, he was also buying coins and bullion from local collectors and investors. Scott realized that he could make a good living buying and selling coins and bullion and gave up his career as a mortgage broker. Shortly after starting the coin store, he needed some extra help so he recruited his wife to quit her job as an accountant and assist at the store.

By 2003, Scott had an idea to see if he could sell bullion coins and bars online, just like the "big dealers" at the time like KITCO or the now-bankrupt Bullion Direct. He scraped together around $10,000, which was a large sum of money to him and hired some web development contractors to build his first website, which was ready in April of 2003.

Scott's business was previously named "CheaperGold.com" thinking that he could attract price-conscious buyers to buy from his little website as opposed to shopping from the giants. Scott was more successful than even he had imagined. CheaperGold.com became APMEX and a giant was born.

As the old saying goes, "Timing, in life, is everything." Scott's timing could not have been better. Americans were starting to search the web, by the millions, in order to buy products. Online shopping was just starting to become a way of life for busy people and those in more remote locations. From your living room, bedroom, office, you were able to comparison shop by comparing prices against one another. It was like having a coin show in your living room.

But it was more than timing that made APMEX successful. It was a vision of what Scott wanted APMEX to be. He actually had two visions for the company. First he wanted the company to have an unparalleled inventory so that customers would not need to search everywhere for the specific products that they wanted. That would be an expensive proposition—but one that he knew would drive more business to the company.

His second vision was even more important. Scott wanted the customer experience to be primarily online, which would be less costly, but still offer customers a friendly and knowledgeable voice on a telephone should the customer be more comfortable buying in that manner. He wanted the customer experience to be much better than what customers were currently experiencing buying bullion and coins online. He dreamt of a customer experience where the customer gets knowledge and **transparent pricing**.

Let me tell you about pricing in the coin and bullion business. Back then, the buy prices that you would receive from many dealers, if you were perceived as unknowledgeable, were price offers that were as low as possible but could still be justified. If you were a more experienced seller, or a small dealer, you received a higher price offer. With many of the dealers at the time, the more that you knew, the better deal you would get.

Scott didn't care much for that philosophy. Instead, he began listing his basic bullion items with BOTH a BUYING price and a SELLING price! That transparency was revolutionary in the bullion market. No one else was offering to tell you what they would pay for a Krugerrand as well as what their selling price was—for everyone. Scott had leveled the playing field for buyers of bullion items!

By 2005, APMEX had hit a major milestone. APMEX had just acquired their 10,000th customer and business was active. By 2006, APMEX reached another milestone—40,000 orders shipped to their customers by their 40 employees.

To better establish the APMEX name, the company branded their own gold and silver product lines in 2007. With the gold market heating up and the spot price climbing to $1,000, APMEX grew to 62 employees in 2008.

I must digress here. In March of 2008, Scott had invited me to come down to Edmond, Oklahoma, wherever that was, and to

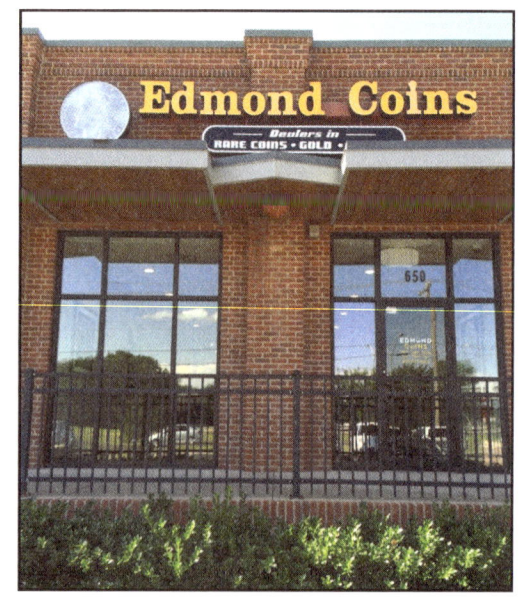

(APMEX started as a small coin shop in Edmond, called Edmond Coins. This is what I saw after flying 1,500 miles. Although it looked nice, I was not much impressed. Photo courtesy of Edmond Coins.)

see his operation. I reluctantly went and was given directions to follow on how to get to APMEX. One of my directions was that I was to look for a small coin shop, called Edmond Coins, in a strip mall. After my long flight from Boston, I drove and was able to find Edmond Coins. To be brutally honest, I was not very impressed. This looked like a very small operation to be candid.

I thought to myself, well maybe Scott will buy me lunch, and since the entire trip was on his dime, I tried to make the most of it. I expected a more impressive operation than just a small coin shop.

Disappointed, I still walked in at the appointed time, spoke to an employee in the coin shop and met with Scott. He took me back through the coin shop to the center of the strip mall. Behind locked doors were vaults, a Sales Department, an Accounting Department, a Marketing Department and an Operations Department. With approximately 60 employees, APMEX was growing fast and the bullion market was cooperating with that growth. This is EXACTLY what I wanted to see.

I met people who were extremely busy not only because the market was strong but also because customers were flocking to APMEX in droves. The market movement meant that APMEX had more business than it could handle. Scott needed people to help his business grow on its upwards trajectory and that day I spent more than 12 hours with him.

I was impressed with what I saw. A small but rapidly-growing company where the owner knew everyone and they all liked what they were doing. They were extremely busy but that was the result of two factors—an incredibly active market and their guiding principles that Scott had instilled—passion for his business, transparent pricing, unmatched selection and unparalleled customer service. I could see he had a winning combination here—but he needed more people with experience to help the company grow. I knew that I wanted to be part of this company's likely success. I joined APMEX in June of 2008 and APMEX grew from 40,000 customers in 2005 to over 100,000 customers by the end of 2008.

(Scott Thomas and the team at APMEX standing in front of The Reserve Building in Oklahoma City, OK. Photo courtesy of APMEX.)

In March of 2009, Scott made me his VP and together we helped the company tackle new challenges and grow like crazy. APMEX became one of only 13 companies worldwide that could buy silver bullion products direct from the U.S. Mint as an "Authorized Purchaser." APMEX had been purchasing products from the Perth Mint for years and now we focused on building relationships with many other sovereign mints to provide their products to APMEX's customers. We were also selling and shipping to dozens of foreign countries. The bullion market was really moving upwards very fast as well.

By the end of 2010, APMEX had garnered over ONE BILLION dollars in sales—a feat matched by only a tiny handful of companies in this industry. By 2012, APMEX had shipped its unbelievable 1,000,000th order and we simultaneously launched Citadel Global Depository Services, a joint venture with Brinks, with me as its first President. Citadel would offer storage options by Brinks for physical precious metals.

One additional major positive change for APMEX in 2010 was the move of the company from its humble origins in Edmond, Oklahoma. APMEX was proud to announce the relocation of its business to the 80,000 square foot Federal Reserve Bank Building in Oklahoma City. The move took several months to complete and the use of numerous armored cars to transfer the valuable cargo to the new location.

Built in 1922 of 3-foot thick Indiana limestone, the "Reserve Building" was a fortress that was built by the Federal Reserve system. APMEX loved the idea that the massive vaults that protected the Federal Reserve's gold and silver in the 1920s for more than 70 years, would now protect APMEX's gold and silver into the future. It was a perfect marriage of high-technology protecting valuable precious metal assets inside of a nearly 100-year-old seemingly impenetrable fortress.

But APMEX kept growing bigger and bigger, even after the bullion prices retrenched in 2013. Gold dropped from a high of $1,833 per ounce in 2012 to $1,245 in 2013 but the company continued its growth. Encouraged by APMEX Senior Management, eBay sought an online trading relationship with APMEX to bring stability to their bullion marketplace and the APMEX Bullion Center on eBay was born!

(The APMEX Bullion Center on eBay was created in 2013 – Photo courtesy of CoinWeek.)

In 2014, APMEX won approval from the Oklahoma legislature to successfully pass a sales tax exemption for bullion and numismatic coins. I worked closely with Scott and our lobbyists to make this a reality and APMEX grew to shipping its products to 83 countries around the globe. By 2015, the products listed on the APMEX website exceeded more than 10,000 choices. APMEX passed the 460,000 clients mark and we were named #46 of the Top 500 E-Retailers in all of North America.

As other precious metals companies' business slowed, APMEX kept charging ahead. 2016 saw APMEX as the #42 Internet E-Retailer and APMEX completed that year with $7.75 billion dollars in lifetime bullion transactions. By 2018, APMEX had launched their own minting facility, called 9Fine Mint, as well as created a partnership with Sprott Ltd. to establish a marketplace for digital precious metals called OneGold.

I retired from APMEX in 2019 but have continued to be amazed by its growth regardless of the market conditions. My love for the company that I served and my colleagues continues to this day.

WHAT'S SO GREAT ABOUT APMEX

Hundreds of thousands of customers have put their trust in APMEX. They feel confident that every product they buy from APMEX is genuine, has been checked for authenticity, is priced competitively and has been purchased from a reliable source.

With APMEX, what you see is what you get. The pricing is clear and transparent. There are no hidden fees or charges (your state may require sales tax) and you get what you have ordered.

Unlike some other online retailers, APMEX will not call you and try to separate you from your money! If you ask an APMEX representative to call you when an item reaches a certain price or some item is back in stock, they would be happy to do so. But they are not going to bother you with unsolicited sales calls. That is NOT the "APMEX Way!"

Likewise, if you want suggestions as to what to buy the Representatives are there to help you. They will offer suggestions to help you buy what you like or to buy what will help diversify your portfolio, they are happy to make suggestions and to help you understand your options. They want you to be happy with your purchase and they stand behind what they sell.

Clearly, there is a reason why APMEX has grown from that small coin shop to a retail outlet, to a massive company that sells BILLIONS of dollars of products each year and requires more than 200 employees to support the business. Other players in the precious metals arena have grown but not to the extent that APMEX has.

It all goes back to Scott Thomas' vision of unparalleled inventory choices, competitive prices and treating you, the customer, with care, courtesy and respect. Scott's team has added features on the APMEX website that complement his philosophy. These features help you stay informed and make good investment decisions.

For customers APMEX allows you to keep your precious metals portfolio online, where its prices are updated automatically. In this way you always know the value of your precious metal holdings. Automated Market Alerts can send text messages direct to your smartphone to advise you when your favorite precious metal(s) reach your specific price points in the market. This can help you take advantage of selling opportunities. APMEX will watch the market for you, so you can continue with your busy life.

Do you want to buy specific products at specific prices? You can easily do that without watching the market day in and day out. By simply setting pricing alerts, you will know when it is time for you to react to what is happening in the market. And they do all the watching for you!

Another great feature is APMEX's exclusive AlertMe feature which allows you to be notified when your favorite APMEX products are back in stock. It gives you a sneak peek of the APMEX inventory before others are even aware of it.

There are HUNDREDS of THOUSANDS of words of education on the APMEX website so becoming an informed consumer is not only possible but likely!

One additional important feature that I want to call your attention to is for certified coin buyers. If you are buying a certified (PCGS or

NGC-graded) coin for your collection, you would like to know how many have been certified at that grade, how many exist in a higher grade, as well as the total mintage of that specific coin. Prior to the creation of COIN**GRADE**+ (Coin Grade Plus) you would have had to search the web for all of that specific information. APMEX has done the work for you and put all of that information at YOUR fingertips.

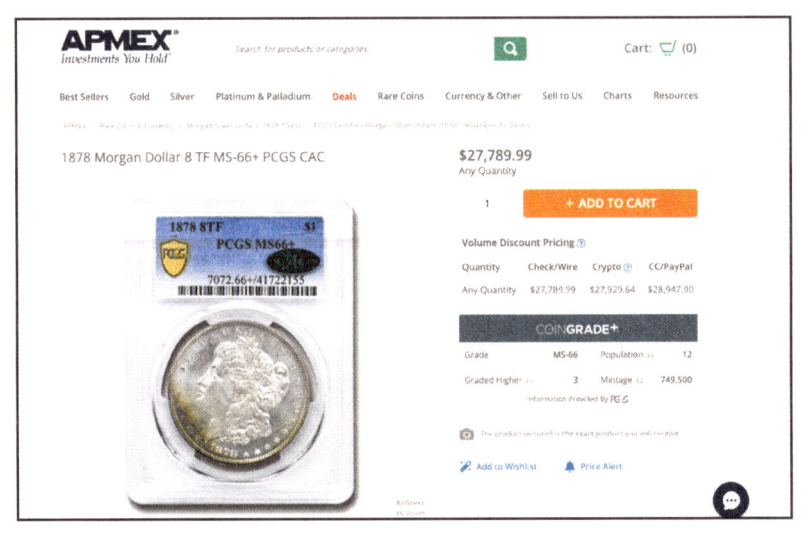

*(Coin**Grade**+ is a feature you will only find at APMEX – saving you time and money and helping you make better investment decisions. Photo courtesy of APMEX.)*

Bells and whistles are really nice to have and to use at your convenience. But the proof of a company's value comes when a mistake has occurred. If you are like APMEX and ship hundreds of thousands of packages annually, some small number of mistakes will unfortunately occur. Even with the most careful of checking and with redundant verification systems in place, APMEX people are human beings and everyone makes the occasional mistake.

The proof of your worth comes when you do make that mistake and how you then treat the customer and rectify the situation. APMEX always tries to give customers the benefit of the doubt and they are never "too big, too important" to acknowledge their mistake and apologize for your inconvenience.

APMEX employees are people, like you, who appreciate the value that gold and silver can bring and like you, they work hard to do a good job—for YOU. They want YOUR business. Whether you can spend $1,000 a year or $10 million, every customer is truly important to APMEX and every customer receives that same care and respect.

YOU CAN TRUST APMEX!

That is what separates APMEX from the rest of the bullion crowd.

After spending more than 11 years at APMEX I am proud to say that I worked for APMEX. Coming to Oklahoma, even at that late stage in my career, was the right thing for me to do. And after spending more than 40 years in this industry I know the bullion and coin companies that treat customers well and put customers first.

APMEX leads that list, in my humble opinion. I will make this statement because I truly believe it, "You can trust APMEX!"

(APMEX employees pulling products for your order. Photo courtesy of APMEX.)

SECRETS OF THE RARE COIN AND BULLION BUSINESS

(Scott Thomas, President and Founder of APMEX [left] and the author [right]. Photo courtesy of APMEX.)

(The APMEX website - Photo courtesy of APMEX.)

08 | BLACK SWAN EVENTS

WHAT THE HECK IS A BLACK SWAN EVENT?
Investopedia – the online dictionary for investors, describes a "Black Swan" event as follows:

> "A **black swan** is an unpredictable **event** that is beyond what is normally expected of a situation and has potentially severe consequences. **Black swan events** are characterized by their extreme rarity, their severe impact, and the widespread insistence they were obvious in hindsight."

Some examples of a "Black Swan" event are the terrorist bombings on September 11, 2020 and, more recently, the Coronavirus pandemic that affected the stock market from March through May of 2020.

ANOTHER PEARL HARBOR
Tuesday, September 11, 2000, was another day that "will live in infamy," just like the surprise attack on Pearl Harbor. A clear, sunny, beautiful September morning turned ugly as first one and then a

second plane crashed into the World Trade Center in New York City. When the first plane hit at 8:46 AM, everyone was wondering—"How could this happen? How could a passenger aircraft hit a skyscraper with all of today's (2000) technology?" It must have been a terrible accident or some type of loss of control.

But when the second plane hit at 9:04 AM, everyone watching suddenly realized that this was no accident. It was deliberate. It was an act of war on peaceful citizens. When Pearl Harbor was bombed, it was an attack on our military. When 9/11 occurred, it was an attack on American citizens.

The New York Stock Exchange (NYSE), the London Stock Exchange and other exchanges around the world closed once we all realized that this was no accident. The New York Exchange was closed for four days. That was the longest closure since 1933. When the NYSE reopened, it was chaos!

The market reopened on Monday, September 17th. Stock and bond investors were understandably rattled by the earth-shattering events, and the Dow Jones Industrial Average (DJIA) closed the day down 7.13%. That first day of trading (Monday, September 17th) following the September 11th atrocity represented the single worst day in the DJIA history, up to that point in time, in terms of percentage of points lost. The DJIA dropped 864 points and the Standard and Poor's' 500 (S&P 500) Index fell 15%!

Gold prices shot up like a rocket from $215 per troy ounce to $287 per troy ounce in the 6 days from September 11th to September 17th. It was in demand as scared investors sold everything they could sell and turned their investments into cash. Gold was greatly in demand all around the world and the physical metals couldn't meet the demand for several weeks. As more manufacturers produced more and the fever-pitch demand was being met with supply, precious metal prices stabilized.

The wars in Afghanistan and Iraq would soon follow as the United States needed to avenge the deaths of 3,000 innocent Americans.

Precious metals supply soon caught up with demand and gold stabilized at around $300 per troy ounce.

A MAN'S HOME IS HIS... ALBATROSS

As the war in the Middle East dragged on, other factors came into play to create yet another seminal event—but this one took much more time to play out as opposed to the 9/11 attacks. As some Americans were busy fighting a war in the Middle East, banks and mortgage lenders were busy making money hand over fist. How?

Tax policy played a role in that if you continued to buy more expensive houses you could roll your gains over and over and over without realizing them until you retired. As the mortgage brokers caught onto this, predatory lending schemes allowed many more people to obtain larger and larger mortgages, whether they could ultimately afford them or not. Soon the big banks joined the small mortgage lenders in offering these risky sub-prime mortgages. Interest rates were extremely low and everyone could qualify for a nice big mortgage. The dot-com tech bubble of the 1990s became the housing boom of the 2000s.

Housing prices peaked in 2006, and the crash of 2007 and 2008 soon followed. Suddenly houses were worth less than the balances on their mortgage statements. Loan defaults and bankruptcies soon followed in record numbers. The economy was in shambles...

But of course, what is bad news for most American investors and home owners is good news for precious metal owners. Gold prices rose almost as fast as housing prices dropped. In 2001 (post-9/11) the gold price was a bit over $400 per troy ounce. By 2006, gold had climbed to $859 and during 2007, it reached a high of $985. During the peak in 2008, it climbed further up over $1,000 per troy ounce.

Even after the housing market settled, the bankruptcies still continued to climb as most every American was feeling the pressure of sub-prime mortgages. By August of 2011, gold peaked at over $1,900 per troy ounce. Premiums were at all-time highs and dealers had little inventory to sell. Demand for all gold products outstripped the supply. But demand slowed in 2012 and profit-taking became the norm.

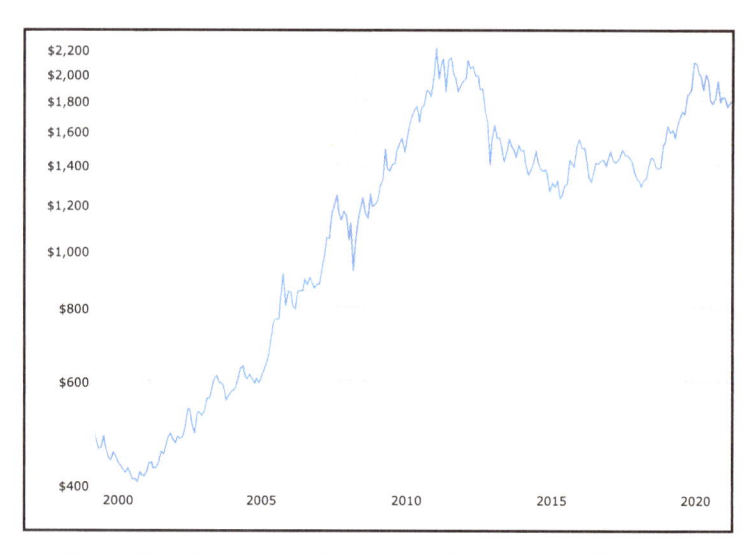

(A Chart of Gold Prices from 2000 to 2020. Chart courtesy of MacroTrends www.macrotrends.net)

Precious metal premiums went up and up and up during 2006 to 2011, but by 2013, even the gold bubble had burst and supplies were now outstripping the demand.

YOU CAN'T SELL WHAT YOU DON'T OWN

Having inventory for a precious metal dealer is critical. You cannot sell what you do not have. Over my 40+ years in the industry I have experienced and lived through all kinds of coin and precious metal shortages. Sometimes its silver, other times gold, occasionally platinum or palladium. But it usually never is all four of the major metals at once.

History—meet the Coronavirus pandemic of 2020. This "perfect storm" hit the United States in March of 2020 and turned the world on its ear. And that certainly included the precious metals market too. Travel was suspended, manufacturing was suspended, the virus circled the globe and the United States paid a particularly heavy price for being virtually unprepared.

As of the writing of this article (August 2020) over 18 million people world-wide have been affected, with 690 thousand deaths, including over 158 thousand in the U.S. alone. Unemployment, due to the virus and the mandatory closing of non-essential businesses and stores, reached Great Depression-like levels. By the end of May, over 40 million Americans had filed for unemployment.

Precious metal products in Asia, Europe and in South America were unable to travel to the United States to satisfy the unquenchable thirst for gold and silver. This was precipitated by wild swings in the U.S. stock market wreaking havoc on retirement accounts and retired individuals. For example, on March 9, 2020, as the death toll from the Coronavirus was reaching very disturbing levels, the Dow Jones Industrial Average (DJIA) suffered a **2,213 POINT DROP!** That translated to a 7.8% loss in value for the 30 Blue Chip stocks that comprise the DJIA. In one single day!

Was that an aberration—a one-day loss that would never recur again?

Ummmm... no. On March 12th—just 3 days later, the Dow dropped another 2,353 points or nearly 10%. And on March 16th the Dow dropped another 2,297 points for a loss now of 12.93% of its value. In those three trading days alone, the Dow lost nearly 30% of its value. Historic is not the right word to describe it. Terrifying is much closer to how investors felt. Yes, there were corrections in both directions but the damage had been done.

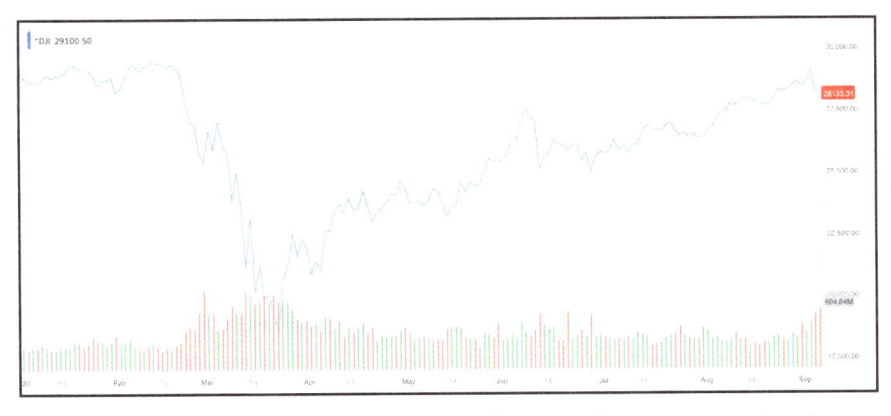

(The DJIA volatility in March of 2020 due to the Coronavirus was unprecedented. Chart courtesy of Yahoo!Finance.)

Investor confidence in the safety of the U.S. stock markets was shaken to its core.Unlike other Black Swan events, this one made the supplies of product "quarantine at home" so there was a shortage in the marketplace that only grew and grew and grew as demand continued to increase.

The stock market volatility had investors fleeing as quickly as possible. But where could they put their cash that escaped the repeated crashes in the stock market? Why in precious metals of course!

The immediate demand for precious metals not only drove prices (and premiums) higher and higher but the demand quickly outstripped the available supply. Bullion dealer after bullion dealer stopped selling products or was unable to offer any meaningful numbers of products to customers trying to buy anything and everything they could find.

For example, APMEX at the beginning of March of 2020 had nearly 25,000 products in stock and ready for immediate delivery. The first wave of crashes took out any gold or silver products with low to average premiums. The longer this kept happening the more products flew off the shelves. Soon less than 10,000 were still on the shelves and bullion products were few and far between.

While that sounds great for most precious metals dealers, it posed a huge problem. How do you replace these products in a market where the newly-created supplies (in Asia, in Europe, across the United States) cannot get to you. Americans, except those in essential jobs, were told to stay home, to work from home and not to travel. Air flights were limited or often suspended. Shipments of precious metal products coming from overseas were quarantined for 14 days, or longer, to stop the Coronavirus.

And dealers and manufacturers wanted higher and higher premiums for their products. In order to have anything available for sale, precious metal traders paid higher and higher premiums to try to maintain some level of inventory and to have products to offer to customers. The demand and the inability to manufacture products and get them into the market in a timely manner were unprecedented! Many precious metal dealers offered very few, if any, products. In April, I spoke with a representative of a major, well-known sovereign mint and asked him what he had for sale.

He had a grand total of two, yes two, different products that he could offer me. One was a platinum product and the other was a gold product with a very high premium due to licensing, and due to the short supply of ANY products in the marketplace.

Through it all, a number of precious metals dealers attempted to remain open. Most precious metals dealers that had products of any kind remained open, as an essential business and took numerous precautions—masks, social distancing, limited personnel interactions, staggered work shifts—to protect their employees and to keep products coming into the marketplace. The precious metals dealer community stayed open as long as they could get products to sell.

The market has yet to return to normal. Demand keeps gold and silver prices moving higher and higher.

YOU WANT HOW MUCH?

The Coronavirus has changed the precious metals landscape, at least for now. Premiums are higher because demand is still outstripping supply. Should the virus surging stop and manufacturers begin to routinely deliver products we could see prices relax a bit but until the demand abates, prices may continue to rise.

Even during these times of unpredictable price swings in the bullion markets, all precious metals dealers are trying to keep items in stock and keep their prices highly competitive. But the lack of inventory makes that difficult at best.

Pricing products is always difficult when there is an unpredictable supply.

These historic price movements not only affected gold but silver as well, though silver is not near a historic high, it has moved up in price considerably.

SECRETS OF THE RARE COIN AND BULLION BUSINESS

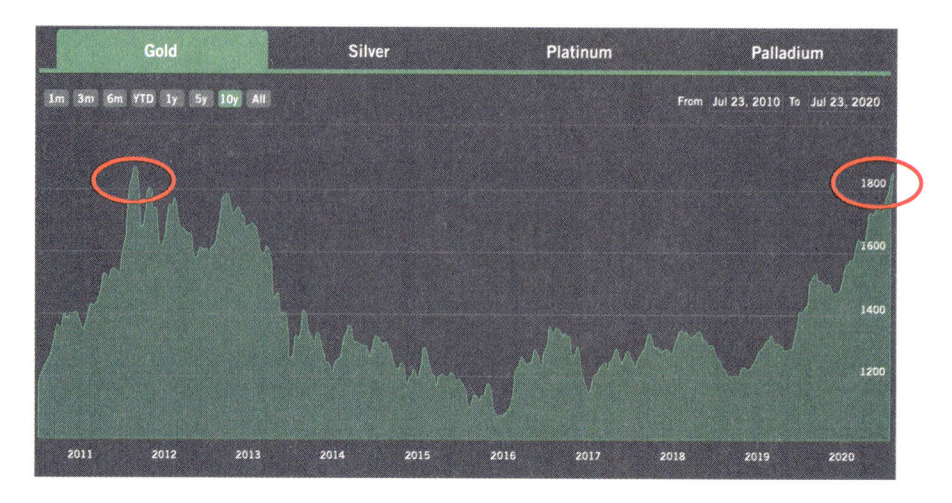

(This 10-Year Gold Price Chart shows how close prices are today (July 23, 2020) to all-time highs that occurred in September of 2011. Gold Chart courtesy of APMEX.)

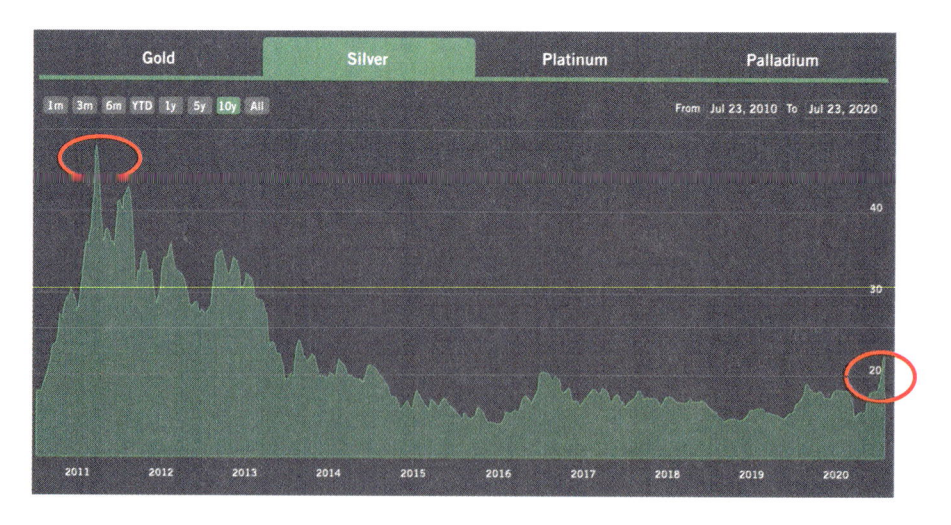

This Silver Price Chart Shows that Silver is NOT near its historic High in April of 2011, but demonstrates that it has moved up considerably this year, due, in part to the Coronavirus and due to very strong demand. Silver Price Chart Courtesy of APMEX.)

Silver demand is strong as it has a low bar to entry. The silver to gold ratio today is approximately 83:1, which means it takes 83 ounces of silver to equal the price of one ounce of gold. The ratio hit 100:1 earlier in July before the metals started this climb.

Pricing is one component why customers buy from a certain dealer. Look for dealers that price their products competitively. There may be dealers who can sell a silver product for ten cents cheaper or a dollar or two cheaper on gold than the average price. But price is only part of the equation.

Quick and safe delivery, direct communications, and reliability are all other considerations when buying online. Some companies will not offer products that it doesn't have in its inventory as many other dealers do. Look at what each dealer is offering you—beyond just the price!

HOW TO BE PREPARED

Now you know all about Black Swan events. You can see that when they happen the same usual factors come into play—a drop in the stock market or a drop in housing prices. This is followed, almost simultaneously, by a strong increase in precious metals prices and a strong increase in demand.

Not all precious metals will go up or down the same amount or to the same degree. So it makes perfect sense to start your buying program while the market is stable. So, what can I do to be prepared?

First thing you should do is create a plan. Look at your stocks, bonds, money market instruments. Make certain that you have cash for emergencies. Make certain that you have enough cash for paying your bills should you become unemployed.

Now once those emergency needs are addressed, calculate what you can invest, outside of the conventional investment markets. Let's say you have $200,000 in investments and $25,000 in emergency cash. Now it is time to decide how much you want/need to have in precious metals. Let's assume you want a 20% position in precious metals. That translates to approximately $56,000 in Precious Metals.

Of that $56K, you should divide it, evenly, and spend approximately $28k in gold and a like amount in silver. So what do I buy?

Buy what you personally like best—whether it is Silver Eagles, silver rounds or silver bars. Know that Silver Eagles will have the highest premium because they tend to always be in the greatest demand. Or buy what has the lowest premium so you get more silver for your dollar. Or buy what is available as silver is still in short supply. It isn't that difficult to spend money on precious metal items. But buy what YOU like.

Make a plan to buy a specified amount per week. Then buy that amount. If the dealer you like to shop with offers free shipping over $100 or $500, make sure you spend that amount. Or if the dealer has volume discount model buy at the discounted levels.

Here is an example of volume discount pricing:

VOLUME DISCOUNT PRICING		QUICKSHIP® ELIGIBLE	
QUANTITY	CHECK/WIRE	BTC/BCH	CC/PAYPAL
1–19	$29.79	$30.10	$31.03
20–99	$29.29	$29.60	$30.51
100–499	$28.79	$29.09	$29.99
500–999	$28.29	$28.58	$29.47
1,000+	$27.79	$28.08	$28.95

(A typical Volume Discount Pricing Model. Courtesy of APMEX.)

In this example, do not buy one of the coins if you can afford to buy 25. You will save 50 cents per coin if you can buy 25 and that translates to a savings of $12.50. Likewise do not use a credit card or PayPal to buy these coins because at 24 or less you will pay $1.24 more on each coin.

Study your options. Consider buying enough to get volume discounts and shop around!

BUYING THROUGH THE D-C-A METHOD

Okay so what is the D-C-A method of Buying? It stands for Dollar-Cost-Averaging and it is explained by Investopedia as:

> **WHAT IS DOLLAR-COST AVERAGING (DCA)?**
> Dollar-cost averaging (DCA) ia an investment strategy in which an investor divides up the total amount to be invested across periodic purchases of a target asset in an effort to reduce the impact of volatility on the overall purchase. The purchases occur regardless of the asset's price and at regular intervals; in effect, the strategy removes much of the detailed work of attempting to time the market in order to make purchases of equities at the best prices. Dollar-cost averaging is also known as the constant dollar plan.

(Dollar-Cost –Averaging Description – Courtesy of Investopedia. https://www.investopedia.com/)

Contrary to what investment advisors might tell you, no one knows for certain whether the market will move up or down and when that will happen. They might be good at guessing on a specific day or two but that's the best that anyone can hope for.

Dollar-cost-averaging takes the guess work out of trying to time the market. Your average of all of your buys quite often will be better than if you just bought all of your allocation in one trading session. You might get lucky and buy on a low point but that is all it is—getting lucky.

The strategy of diversifying your investments, buying using volume discounts and using the dollar-cost-averaging method of when to buy is a sound philosophy to follow for acquiring your precious metals.

Once you have them, keep them safe and YOU, too, will be ready for the next Black Swan event.

(Black Swan events are waiting for YOUR investments.)

09 | TO CAC OR NOT TO CAC?

WHAT IN THE WORLD IS CAC?

Certified Acceptance Corporation, or CAC for short, is a company that was founded in 2007 and is based in Far Hills, NJ. The idea for CAC was based upon a simple premise—that not all NGC and PCGS coins are alike, even if they share the same certified grade. There are coins that are "especially nice for the grade" and there are coins that may be "under-graded by at least one point." For a fee, CAC identifies these coins and affixes a small green sticker—signifying high-end quality for the grade, or a gold sticker—signifying under-graded by at least a point, to the front of the NGC or PCGS slab. Or if your coin doesn't meet CAC's idea of a high-end or under-graded coin, it is simply returned to you—without a CAC bean. So, does that mean PCGS and NGC coins are incorrectly graded to begin with? NO!

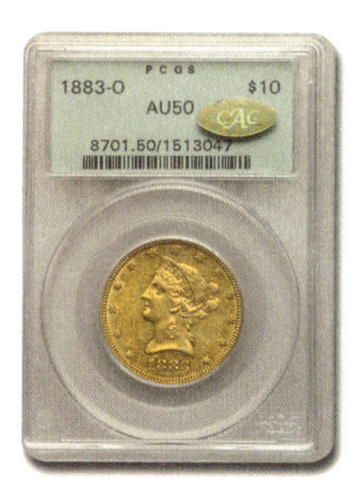

(An NGC-graded Peace Silver Dollar with a Green CAC sticker [left] and an older, OGH [old green holdered] PCGS-graded $10 Gold Liberty with a Gold CAC sticker [right]. Photos courtesy of APMEX.)

The premise is that is any knowledgeable dealer or collector, who is adept at accurately grading coins, can look at ten 1881-S Morgan silver dollars, all of which are graded MS65 by NGC or PCGS, and then that dealer/collector could put them in some order from nicest to worst for the grade.

CAC looks at PCGS and NGC graded coins and determines if the coin is nicer than average or under-graded and affixes the sticker to the holder. For many different types of coins, having CAC approval generates a premium over what a non-CAC coin would bring (More on pricing later).

A SHORT HISTORY OF CERTIFIED COINS

The idea of an independent, 3rd party rendering an opinion on your coins originally started with the American Numismatic Association's Certification Service (ANACS for short) back in 1972. ANACS was originally created to combat the scourge of counterfeit gold coins coming to the United States from the Middle East.

For a fee, ANACS would review the coin that you submitted, determine its authenticity, and assign a numerical grade (or grades) to your coin, employing the Sheldon grading scale. ANACS would take a black and white photograph of each side of your coin and return your coin and photographs to you. ANACS would assign a grade to the obverse and to the reverse of your coin. If the obverse of the coin was nicer than the reverse, one might receive a photo certificate with a "split grade" on the coin of something like MS65/63. This tended to make it more difficult to determine the coins value for these split graded coins. How would you accurately grade a common date Morgan Dollar where it had been ANACS graded as MS63/67? Average it at 64? 65?

Another issue was that a black and white certificate photograph of a silver, untoned, and relatively mark-free coin is difficult to match to the original coin. More than one ANACS photo certificate was sold without the correct corresponding coin attached.

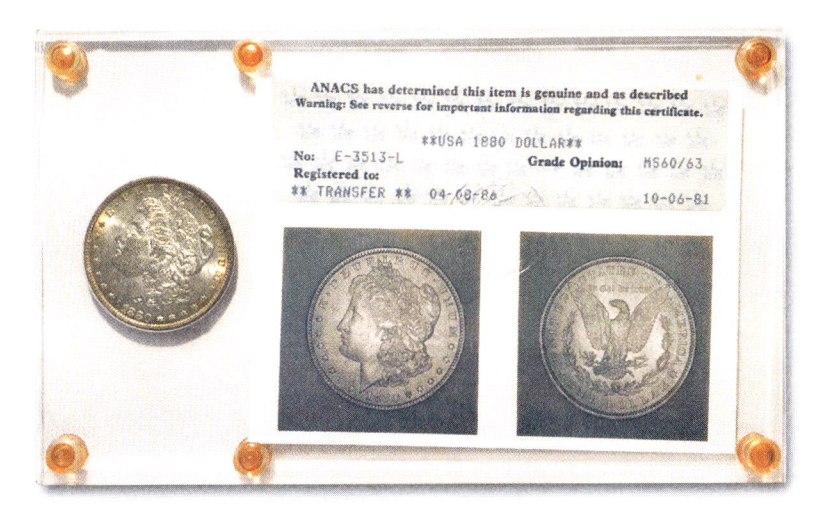

(ANACS Photo-certificates were the granddaddy of 3rd Party Independent coin grading. Note the MS60/63 grades. Photo courtesy of APMEX.)

These photo-certificates didn't stop the unscrupulous from switching a higher grade coin for a lower grade coin, so ANACS developed a "certified holder" that now encapsulated the coin and the assigned grade. But this came after the other major, independent 3rd party grading services were in business and had perfected their holders. Some of the variations on the new ANACS certified holder were as follows:

(As counterfeiting of coins in certified holders, and counterfeiting the holders themselves, became more of an issue from China, all of the major grading services kept on refining their holders to stay one step ahead of the counterfeiters. Photos courtesy of APMEX.)

ANACS is still in business today, but it is no longer owned by the American Numismatic Association. It is still considered to be a reputable grading service, but it is not in the top-tier.

There's nothing like a good idea to bring out imitators. James Halperin, the genius behind New England Rare Coin Galleries in the 1980s, formed a partnership with Steve Ivy and together they created the powerhouse today that is Heritage Auctions (www.HA.com). But in the 1980s Halperin wrote a book on grading coins and he went a step further and created a company called Numismatic Certification

Institute (NCI). NCI graded coins but they took color pictures and put the grades on the color certificates.

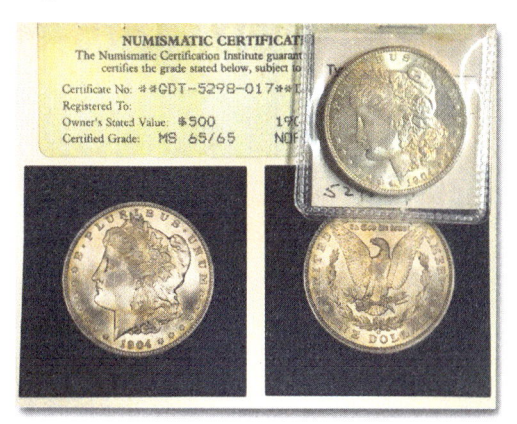

(The NCI Photo-Certificate in color [left], was later replaced by the NCI Slab [right]. Photos courtesy of the Author.)

Along the way, literally dozens (hundreds?) of independent third party coin grading services came along. It's an alphabet soup of acronyms and impressive sounding names—Accugrade, Independent Coin Graders, Hallmark, Photo-Certified Coin Institute (PCI), Sovereign Entities Grading Service (SEGS), NumisTrust (NTC), American Coin Grading service (ACGS), Dominion Grading Service (DGS), International Numismatic Bureau (INB), Premier Coin Grading and Authentication (PCGA), Professional Grading Service (PGS) and dozens more.

Some of these companies are still in business, many are not. Some had questionable grading others strived for accuracy and consistency. But this bring us to the two GIANTS of independent, third-party grading—PCGS and NGC.

The Professional Coin Grading Service (PCGS) began operations in 1986. The company was started by David Hall and six other coin dealers. A PCGS dealer there at the very start of the company, was John Albanese of New Jersey (more on John later in this chapter).

The idea behind PCGS was to eliminate many of the abuses that were prevalent in the industry at the time. Without a consistent and accurate grading standard, dealers could call a coin any grade that they wanted—and could price it however they wanted as well. Many telemarketing firms sold horribly over-graded coins to investors who wanted to diversify their portfolios and to take advantage of a market that seemed to do well when the stock market did not. PCGS, for a fee, would grade your coin, by a consensus of their graders, and you would be charged the same fee regardless of the grade. In that way, PCGS made the same grading fee whether your coin was low grade or a higher grade.

In addition, PCGS was building a network of larger, more well-capitalized dealers, who would make a bid on your PCGS-graded coins on a SIGHT-UNSEEN basis. That meant greater liquidity for the investor or collector and surety that their coins were accurately graded. If PCGS over-graded your coin, they would buy it back or financially compensate you. They believed in their products and in their grading.

Some dealers resisted becoming a PCGS dealer or having their coins certified. I remember doing a coin show in Dallas, Texas, in 1987, where a dealer who was set up next to my table leaned over as I was placing my newly-graded PCGS slabs in my showcases. The dealer said to me, "next year when you come back here, you will have cracked all of your coins out of those expensive plastic holders. Collectors don't want to pay for plastic!"

I was polite—I didn't argue with him. But I knew he was wrong—dead wrong. Consistent, consensus grading eliminated many of the abuses that had existed in the coin market. No dealer liked paying a fee to have someone else grade their coins. But by having your coins slabbed, it then eliminated the discussion of whether the coin was accurately graded or not. It made coin buying easier and safer for dealers, collectors and investors. Every coin was authenticated before it could be certified.

That dealer wasn't alone. A sizable number of collectors also objected to paying more for a coin because it was in a slab. But a majority of collectors appreciated the fact that grading was now consistent. Some collectors now faced a conundrum. Collectors often liked to put their nice coins into coin albums. So why would I want to pay for all of that plastic and then have to remove their coins from the PCGS holder after buying them? It was (and still is) a perplexing problem!

But the smart collectors knew this was a good thing. Grading coins just got easier since all you had to read the grade assigned by PCGS on the insert. Many collectors (and some smart dealers) also loved to improve their own grading skills by studying these PCGS certified coins—day in and day out, at every coin show they went to. It made the entire market a bit smarter about grading coins.

The early PCGS coin holders were called "rattlers" as they let the coins rattle around inside. But 24, yes 24, versions of the PCGS coin holder later, we now have a micro-chip, security printing measures and other improvements to the PCGS holder. Millions of coin certifications later, PCGS is one of the two undisputed leaders in the world of 3rd party coin grading.

(From top left to right, Early PCGS Coin Holders: Rattler holder, Doily holder, and a Uni-Coin holder.)

But just as Chevrolet needed Ford to compete with them which, over decades, has forced each company to improve their products, PCGS need a competitor and up stepped a new competitor—Numismatic Guaranty Corporation (NGC).

NGC was the brainchild of New Jersey native John Albanese—yes that same John Albanese who was there in the very early days of PCGS. John felt he could do the same thing that PCGS did, but only better.

So NGC competed with PCGS for the dealers' submissions and for the nicest coins on the market. And grade coins they did! Each grading service competed against the other to be the most consistent, the most accurate and the most conservative grading service.

By the year 2000, fully supportive dealer networks had evolved for both PCGS and NGC. The two companies forced each other (and themselves) to keep innovating and making their certified coins more accurate and more consistent. Each company added features and continually evolved their respective holders. NGC was the first company to grade world coins and tokens and medals. PCGS followed suit. NGC is still today the only company to develop a consistent method of grading an entire category of coins that are inconsistent to begin with—Ancient Coins—and PCGS does still not grade them. Both companies developed and hired paper money graders and developed certification of U.S. and world currency. While PCGS originally spun off and sold their currency grading to a private party (they have since acquired it back), NGC developed their own currency grading.

NGC developed its own holder to quickly and easily identify from the PCGS graded coins. While PCGS opted for a holder that had a clear or opaque background, NGC first surrounded its certified coins with a black foam holder, but many coins especially copper coins or darkly toned silver coins did not look good surrounded by a black surface. After only a few months, NGC switched to a white core surrounding the coins.

NGC and PCGS each had their perceived strengths and weaknesses and dealers learned by sending coins to both grading services where they could get the biggest bang for their buck—getting the highest grades. By 2005,

(An NGC-graded Morgan Silver Dollar in a very RARE NGC First Generation coin holder. Photos courtesy of Heritage Auctions.)

both NGC and PCGS had each graded tens of millions of coins. These two companies were the undisputed leaders in certified, independent, 3rd party grading.

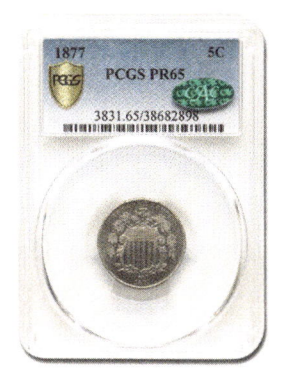

(A PCGS graded Shield Nickel in their newest coin holder [left] and an NGC graded Silver Eagle in their latest holder [right].)

AN IDEA IS BORN

After seeing millions of coins, John Albanese recognized something that other dealers were aware of but no one had developed a way of identifying them. You could place several PCGS or NGC coins, of the same date, mintmark and grade, side-by-side, and you could see that this coin was slightly (or dramatically) better than that one—even though everything about them was the same—grade, date, mintmark. It struck John that he would be able, through his decades of grading expertise, to identify these coins for their owners, for a fee.

John created his next company—Certified Acceptance Corporation (CAC for short) in 2007. It was an immediate success! Everyone wanted their coins to be labeled as a "CAC coin." Coins that received the green bean were immediately identified as premium-quality for the grade—the best of the best! And coins that were under-graded by at least one point, or more, in CAC's estimation, received a gold bean.

I asked John Albanese what was the impetus to start a 3rd party service that picks out high-end or under-graded coins that were already graded by NGC or PCGC. He said that if you think about a more expensive coin, like an MS65 Capped Bust Half Dollar with a Lettered Edge there is a huge spread between certain coins in that grade alone. An average MS65 is approximately $4,000 bid in the Greysheet. But to find one that is high-end for the grade, with lots of eye-appeal, as a dealer you would have to pay $7,500–$8,000 for one. That is because there are coins that make it as an MS65 because of a lack of marks and there are others that are worth premiums well over that $4,000 Greysheet bid. What CAC has done, in John's opinion, has been to level the playing field for investors and collectors. By buying a coin with a CAC sticker on it, you now have a coin that is premium quality for the grade!

Now, PCGS and NGC graded coins would compete in a new arena—for the coveted CAC sticker. Similar to his success with NGC, Albanese had a group of dealers who all wanted to sell high-end (premium quality, better than average, etc.) coins. Not only were they starting to submit coins to CAC, they were hoping that ALL of the coins they submitted to CAC would come back with a green or gold bean on them. They started charging premiums for their own CAC coins and paying premiums to other dealers selling CAC coins. Albanese recognized very rapidly that collectors and investors wanted the nicest coins for their collections too, and CAC helped them instantly spot a high-end coin.

For some collectors, a nice, pleasing average specimen was a great coin for their collection. But for the majority of collectors and investors, having a premium-quality, high-end coin, even for more money, made greater sense. "Buy the best you can afford," is a time-tested adage in the coin business. Dealers and collectors overwhelmingly want to own the nicest coins for their money.

Was this reality? Would dealers pay significant premiums for the really high-end coins in their assigned grades? For many coins—YES! Especially those coins where there are two different market values—a "sight-unseen" price for average NGC/PCGS graded coins and a much stronger "sight-seen" price for above average NGC/PCGS coins.

As a way of validating Albanese's premise, less than 3 years after CAC began operations and started to separate the average coins from the nicer specimens, **both PCGS and NGC jointly announced that**

they were going to start adding a plus sign (+) to coins that they graded that were high-end for the grade! That was one of the very first times that these two competitors announced something jointly. But was that an attempt to end CAC as a business? It had the exact opposite effect. Submissions more than doubled from 4,000 per month to more than 10,000.

It was more like an admission that not all coins are graded equally, even when they are the same grade on their inserts! Albanese had proven, incontrovertibly, that two market prices can exist for coins within the same grade.

This became apparent to dealers and collectors very rapidly. In the very first year of its existence (2007), and without any track record of success determining which coins were high end specimens, CAC had more business than it could comfortably handle. And that business, as well as the numbers of submissions, only continues to grow by leaps and bounds.

CAC now can boast of having more than 830 dealer members and more than 1,300 collector members—along with a waiting list of potential members who want to join. More than 1.5 million coins bear the CAC sticker and the estimated value of those coins is in the BILLIONS of DOLLARS!

But do CAC coins really bring premium prices over their non-CAC counterparts? Well... YES! Now the premiums can range from about

(The CAC sticker, close-up. Photo Courtesy of Certified Acceptance Corp. www.caccoin.com)

a low of 10% to 100% or more, but the coins that have the greatest return are those that are scarce coins to begin with.

CAC coins have brought significant premiums on certain coins in auctions and on bourse floors across America! But not all CAC-stickered coins do as well.

For example, let's look at a few very common "generic" coins:

DATE M/M	DESCRIPTION	GRADE	GREYSHEET BID	CAC BID
1946	Iowa Centennial Commemorative	MS66	$105	$115
1881-S	Morgan Silver Dollar	MS66	$200	$125
1924	$20.00 Saint-Gaudens	MS64	$2,195	$2,295
1945	Walking Liberty Half	MS66	$97	$135
1936	York County Commemorative	MS67	$240	$275
1922	Peace Dollar	MS65	$88	$96
1902-O	Morgan Dollar	MS66	$265	$290
1936	Norfolk Commemorative	MS67	$350	$375
1913-D	Buffalo Nickel, Type II	MS65	$900	$900
1907	$5.00 Gold Liberty	MS63	$595	$645

CAC-stickered coins garnered the same or slightly higher prices, but in many of these instances it is hardly worth the cost and time involved in having these coins CAC certified. And submitting a coin is NO guarantee of obtaining a CAC sticker. But now let's see how more expensive coins fare if they have a CAC sticker versus their non-stickered counterparts.

Here are some better coins and their Greysheet Bids and Greysheet CAC Bids:

DATE M/M	DESCRIPTION	GRADE	GREYSHEET BID	CAC BID
1900	Isabella Quarter Commemorative	MS67	$4,300	$6,300
1922	Grant w/Star Commemorative	MS66	$4,500	$7,000
1926	Sesquicentennial Half Comm.	MS66	$14,000	$19,000
1905	Lewis & Clark $1.00 Gold Comm.	MS65	$3,500	$6,500
1908	$20.00 Saint-Gaudens with Motto	MS65	$9,300	$24,000
1887-S	$20.00 Gold Liberty	MS63	$6,800	$10,000
1910-S	$10.00 Gold Indian	MS64	$8,400	$12,000
1928-S	Peace Dollar	MS65	$9,600	$20,000
1879-O	Morgan Dollar	MS66	$9,000	$16,000
1889-CC	Morgan Dollar	MS64	$60,000	$115,000

The more highly-graded and expensive coins that you have, the greater the difference seems to be between the Greysheet bid and the CAC bid. The CAC bids are posted on the CDN Exchange in live time. CAC is a strong buyer of many of the coins that it approves of and adds a green bean (or gold) to the slab so they fully support what they are doing in the marketplace.

Few coins submitted attain CAC approval and sticker. They estimate about 20% of all coins submitted may qualify for a GREEN sticker while only 40 coins out of every 1,000 submitted do qualify for a GOLD sticker. So do CAC coins only do well if the coins are very expensive and are sold by dealers?

The answer is... let's look at some very recent auction results...

Here are some snippets of recent, major auction house results, as posted on the CAC website—(www.caccoins.com)

> "On August 3, in consecutive lots, Heritage auctioned two PCGS graded MS65 1871 Two Cent pieces, each with a full mint red (RD) designation. The CAC approved MS65RD 1871 realized $9,600 while the non-CAC coin sold for $4,560, less than half as much."

"In successive lots on August 3, Heritage auctioned three certified MS64 grade 1907 High Relief Saint Gaudens $20 gold coins, each with a 'Wire Edge.' The CAC approved NGC graded MS64 coin realized $30,000. The two PCGS graded MS64 coins, neither of which had a CAC sticker realized $19,800 and $18,000, respectively."

"On August 6, 2020, Stack's Bowers auctioned a CAC approved certified MS64-Brown 1809 large cent for $43,200. On August 15, 2018, when market levels for early copper coins were much higher than they were in August 2020, Stack's Bowers auctioned a PCGS certified MS64-Brown 1809 large cent, without a CAC sticker for $22,800."

"On August 27, Legend auctioned a CAC approved MS67 grade 1946-D Walking Liberty half dollar for $1,821.25. On July 22, Heritage sold a PCGS graded MS67 1946-D Walking Liberty half dollar without a CAC sticker for $660."

CAC coin bids are displayed for a number of different series in the Monthly Greysheet.

(An excerpt from the September 2020 Monthly Greysheet, displaying CAC Bids for MS64–66 Peace Dollars through 1928. Image courtesy of CDN Publications.)

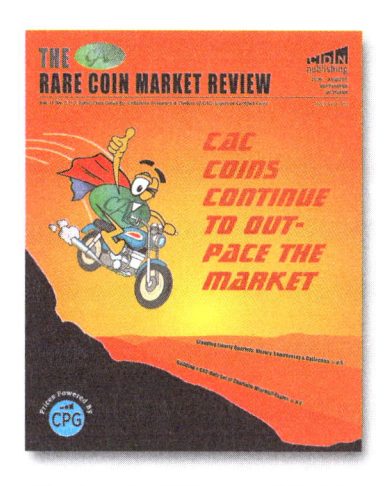

(The Aug–Oct 2020 issue of the CAC Rare Coin Market Review. Image courtesy of CDN Publications.)

Not only can you get your CAC bid prices in the CDN Greysheet, they are also listed electronically on the CDN Exchange.

But if that is not enough for you, there is also a quarterly publication devoted to CAC bid prices. *The CAC Rare Coin Market Review* is published by *the Greysheet*, with prices powered by *The CPG® Coin and Currency Market Review*.

The CAC bids are also posted and can change minute-by-minute on the CDN Exchange. Albanese told me that CAC believes very strongly in the product that they created and in the value it brings to the market for owners of CAC-stickered coins. That is why CAC, itself, is one of the largest market-makers for CAC approved coins and they currently have posted many strong bids.

So are CAC coins for you? It is truly a personal choice and one that you need to consider.

If you are collecting more common, less expensive, "generic" coins, the cost for CAC certification is likely equal to the added value that CAC approval will bring. But for better, scarcer coins or those with tremendous eye-appeal, CAC approval will likely guarantee you a much better return on your numismatic dollar.

10 | WHAT COLLECTORS & INVESTORS NEED TO KNOW

This is probably the most important chapter in this book. If you are a collector or investor and you want to get more enjoyment out of the hobby and make it profitable as well, there are lots of things that you should know.

But these are not my ideas alone. I asked several dealers whom I have known and trusted for many years for their opinions. This is the collective wisdom of over TWO HUNDRED YEARS of experience buying and selling coins. The dealers who participated were:

- **Tom Caldwell**, President of Northeast Numismatics. Tom has been a fixture at all national shows and major coin auctions and he is very knowledgeable on every coin the Red Book. He has more than 50 years of history running his company. His website (www.NortheastCoin.com) is one of the most visited in the industry and offers all U.S. coins, currency and exonumia as well as world coins. In addition to being an ANA life member and a member of the Professional Numismatists Guild (PNG), he is also a member of other regional and national organizations.

- *Jim Carr*, President of Jim Carr, Inc. Jim is extremely knowledgeable about all aspects of United States coins. He has a long family history in the coin business beginning at his uncle's store – Crystal Coin, in Massachusetts, in 1961. He has worked very closely with many collectors helping them build great collections but sells a majority of his inventory wholesale to other dealers. He is a wealth of knowledge on many numismatic topics. He deals in United States and Canadian coins only. His specialties are in early U.S. coins especially Colonials, Half Cents, Large Cents, and Bust Halves. He also specializes in rare, modern varieties, double dies, and errors. He is a Life Member of the ANA and member of other regional organizations.

- *Greg Hannigan*, President of Coin Cube Trading.com (www.CoinCubeTrading.com) and Hannigan's Rare Coins (www.USRareCoinsonline.com). Greg specializes in copper coins and especially Large Cents. He has appeared not only in national coin publications but also in the Wall Street Journal for being the first person to spend more than $1 million on an American penny (a 1795 Large Cent)! Greg is a visionary in this industry. He has built a social media and trading platform unlike any other in the industry. A former combat Marine, Greg is a Life Member of the ANA, a highly respected member of EAC and numerous other numismatic organizations.

- *Kevin Lipton,* President of Kevin Lipton Rare Coins (www.KLRCI.com). Kevin has handled more major rarities of United States coins than most dealers have ever even seen!

His inventory includes some of the finest U.S. rare coins that money can buy. As a teenager, Kevin was considered as a "wunderkind" in the coin business and had his own full-time business at the tender age of 17. Kevin works with some of the most advanced collectors in the country and supplies many large coin dealers. Kevin has handled some of the rarest U.S. coins and has been involved with many of the largest deals in the industry. Kevin received a Life Time Achievement Award from the PNG in 2012. Kevin has sold over $1 billion worth of high quality rare coins.

So what can this distinguished panel tell a collector that is very important for him to know?

KNOWLEDGE IS KING

(I am going to insert the comments of my dealer friends in here and in the subsequent chapter to give you the benefits of their expertise—Enjoy!)

Jim said that "there is another old adage in the coin business—'Buy the book before the coin!' This means you should read about what you want to collect, learn about it. Learn the peculiarities of the coins:

- Do they come well-struck?
- Are the planchets usually perfect?
- Is this coin common or rare?

- Are there many varieties?
- Are the coins in this series available to collect or are they so expensive they are impossible to afford?

Learn as much as you can about what you want to collect. You may wind up knowing more about that series or that particular coin than the dealer selling it to you. And that may be a huge advantage. Many dealers specialize in a series or two but have wider inventories to appeal to more potential buyers."

Greg offered the following advice: "The best advice I can offer a new collector is to read books and become a student of the hobby. Knowledge is king and become knowledgeable about the type of coin or variety you are collecting. Go to shows when you can and research the coins and dealers from whom you would like to start buying.

Learn how to grade the coins you would like to collect. Grading coins is something that takes a long time to learn how to do right, and each coin type or variety has its own challenges.

The metal (from which the coin is comprised) is a large part of learning how to grade, for example, grading copper coins is nothing like grading silver or gold coins.

Try to buy coins that are graded by a third party when possible or with a provenance (a traceable history of ownership).

Join the ANA, EAC, the coin type you wish to collect club, and your local coin club.

Don't be afraid to work long and hard with your hobby, attend coin shows. Go to the meetings and don't be afraid to get to know everyone. Be sure to arrive early, especially at the major coin shows, before Friday, if at all possible.

Be patient and do not make quick decisions on purchases. Becoming a great collector takes time and building a great collection does not always require you to be rich. But it does require you to make smart choices. Those choices will save you money in the end.

Make sure you do your homework about the value of what you wish to collect or buy."

Kevin had some similar ideas. "With the tremendous amount of information available on the internet these days the learning curve is greatly diminished. One can find comps (comps = comparable prices at auction) easily by looking at auction prices realized on the Heritage Auctions website (www.HA.com) and the PCGS web site (www.PCGS.com). There is an endless array of photos of coins to view attached to this auction information. It goes without saying that a novice should only buy coins certified by either PCGS or NGC.

In this day and age there is no need to go to a coin shop or even a coin show—you can buy an amazing amount of coins online. However, the way you build a good relationship with a coin dealer or anyone else for that matter is to be dependable. Follow through on your commitments and don't be difficult to deal with. People always want to do business with those that make it an enjoyable experience. Sounds like a recipe for a good marriage as well!"

Tom offered the following sage advice: "If you are just starting out with strictly the collecting aspect in mind, or are looking to buy for investment, the old tried and true adage still applies—buy the book before the coin. If not a hard copy book, one should at least do the proper research online in advance in the area of that they are interested in.

Try to focus on a particular series so your buying is not too scattered. Another option is to collect by type. For instance, if gold is the area you want to pursue, acquire one of each of the 12 types of U.S. gold coins: Type One, Two, and Three Gold Dollars; Liberty and Indian Quarter Eagles; a Three Dollar Gold piece; Liberty and Indian Half Eagles; Liberty and Indian Eagles; and Liberty and Saint Gaudens Double Eagles.

I would suggest trying to buy the optimum grade in a series which fits within your budget. For example, if you are buying a Saint-Gaudens $20 gold piece, currently a common date in the MS63 to MS64 grade would likely cost you in the $2,200–$2,300 range. However, a nice MS66 grade piece sells for around $3,000. Why settle? This extra outlay of funds should be money well spent in the long term.

I strongly advise that you only buy certified material. These are coins that have been authenticated, graded, and encapsulated by a third-party grading service. Stick with NGC (Numismatic Guaranty Corporation) or PCGS (Professional Coin Grading Service) graded coins. Other grading services do not have the credibility or command the same long-term respect or value as the big two. You should avoid the temptation to stray to what at times may seem like a bargain buy because it's not in an NGC or PCGS holder."

So now with all of this great advice from some of today's smartest dealers, the primary question becomes...

WHAT SHOULD YOU COLLECT?

Buy what YOU like! That is probably the single most important piece of advice that can be given to anyone starting in this hobby. The universe of United States coins run the gamut from Half Cents to Twenty Dollar Gold Coins, from Colonials to Territorial Gold, from Commemorative Coins to Hawaiian Coins, from Patterns to Modern Issues, from Philippines to Alaskan coinage, from Tokens and Medals (also called Exonumia) to Puerto Rican coins, from Ancient coins to world coins, from U.S. to world currency, etc.

How do you know where to start and what to collect?

The simple answer is to collect what YOU like. Buy a current Red Book, and look through it. Study it! Spend several hours with it. Do you like the idea of putting together a set of coins with the same (or similar) obverses and reverses? If so there are MANY series to collect—Half Cents through Twenty Dollar Gold Coins. The possibilities are many and many of the series run for decades! Lincoln cents, for example, began in 1909 (the 100th anniversary of the birth of Abraham Lincoln) and are still being produced today (2020)—111 years later! While other series can be fairly short—Twenty Cent Pieces were first minted in 1875 and the last year of minting was 1878—just four years. But even that series has one coin that will be almost impossible to obtain—1876-CC, with a mintage of only 10,000 coins and a retail price of $175,000 in AU condition. It is a STOPPER!

If you like collecting series of the same coins, then some additional tips for being successful are as follows:

- Pick a series you can complete. Starting a series with many very expensive coins means that you will likely have many holes in your album.
- Buy coins in similar grades and buy the best grade that you can comfortably afford. This allows you to complete the set and have coins that all look similar in the set. A set of Lincoln cents with all of the coins in AU is much nicer and more desirable than a set where conditions run the gamut from Very Good to Mint State. Plus when the time comes to sell the set, it's easier to value for the buyer and easier for you to achieve a better and consistent buying price.
- If you like filling an album that is fine, but on the scarce date coins or more expensive coins—YOU need to decide what is more expensive for YOUR wallet—I would consider buying NGC or PCGS graded coins. And keep them in their holders. Some collectors buy NGC or PCGS graded coins and then crack them out, but save the insert to put them in their album. RESIST THE URGE TO CRACK THEM OUT! Once out of the holders, you have voided the guarantees of authenticity and grade! That extra amount you paid for an NGC or PCGS graded coin is now lost to you!
- Buy a good album to store your coins and have a box for your certified coins—if any. You want to protect the coins and make certain that they do not change their appearance over time by being exposed to air and the elements.

(A nice COMPLETE SET of early Lincoln Cents in Very Fine Condition in a Dansco Album. Photo courtesy of APMEX.)

If you get bored with seeing the same obverse and the same reverses, there are several easy solutions to that. Try something like putting together a 50 piece Classic Commemorative coin type set. This set consists of one of each type of U.S. Commemorative coin issued between 1892 and 1954. Those 50 coins comprise the only quarter commemorative coin—the 1893 Isabella Quarter—the only dollar commemorative coin—the 1900 Lafayette Dollar—and 48 half dollar coins.

What truly makes it interesting is the difference in styles between all of the great coin designers included in this set—Morgan, Fraser, de Francisci, Barber, Sinnock—all designed great circulating coins and all designed great commemorative coins as well.

Some commemorative collectors take it a step further. They collect these coins in their original distribution holders, boxes, envelopes, etc. which is very difficult to do as many of these original holders and scarcer and more valuable than the coins themselves are.

(A 1937 Arkansas P-D-S in Leatherette Box, a 1925 Lexington in Wooden Box, and a pair of 1936 Long Island coins in cardboard holder. Photos courtesy of the author.)

Whatever you decide to collect—U.S. coins, world coins, currency, tokens and medals—make certain it is what YOU like. Don't chase the "hot items" in the market, unless you happen to really like them.

If you decide to collect MS63 NGC-graded Half Cents, or XF Indian Head Cents, try to keep your collection matching as much as possible.

Buy all of the dates (and mintmarks) in the same grade and even by the same grading service if that is possible. The more similar the coins are, the more complete your set will be. If you buy a date in Good and another in XF, the set will look mismatched. So decide before you begin to buy coins which coins look best in which condition and do not settle for lesser grades once you have started your collection, unless the price of a rare or key date coin is out of your price range. Again, the more the set matches, the better the set will look and you should receive better prices overall for your matching collection. A set that is not matched will make the higher grade coins look better but also make the lower grade coins look worse.

A coin collecting adage is "buy the best you can afford." If you can afford to complete a set of Standing Liberty quarters in Very Fine condition, then concentrate on Very Fine condition for all of the coins. But if upgrading all of the coins to AU is still within your wallet's means, then buy all AU coins. Historically, coins in higher circulated grades do better than lower graded coins and the same is true even when the coins are in Mint State.

(On the left is an 1847 Large Cent in Very Good; on the right is an 1847 Large Cent in Extremely Fine. The difference in price between them is $60.00. I know which coin virtually all dealers would prefer to buy. Buy the best you can afford! Photos courtesy of APMEX.)

If you know more about the scarce coins in a series, you may have the advantage over the dealer and your fellow collectors. You may be able to buy scarce varieties of the coins that you have studied as common coins and at common coin prices. And you might not have to pay more for a scarcer variety than for an average specimen. Knowledge is a powerful weapon. It gives you a huge advantage when the time comes to negotiate for a coin. Become a student of the hobby.

READ IT – LEARN IT – REMEMBER IT – BUY IT!

The famous American financier and politician, Russell Sage, is remembered for an important quote that the stock market has adapted for their own use. The quote is "Buy straw hats in December!" Millionaire John D. Rockefeller would often use that quote when people or the press would ask him how he became so wealthy.

What it means is buy something when it is out of season, or in the case of coins—out of favor. The coin market as a whole does not rise and fall together. In fact within different series of coins—Morgan dollars for example, some dates or mintmarks will rise and others will fall at about the same time. In fact, even within certain coins, some grades may go down while other grades of that exact same coin may go up!

Below are the October 2020 Greysheet prices for Barber quarters. Look at the 1893-S date Barber quarter. It is up in MS60, MS62, and MS63. But it is down in MS64 and MS65. And the date below it—1894 is static in MS60 through MS63 but up in MS64 and MS65! A green up arrow means the price has gone up since last month while a red down-pointing arrow means the price is down.

(Prices from the October 2020 Greysheet for Barber Quarters. Courtesy of CDN.)

You can see from the snippet above that prices in certain dates/mintmarks go up in certain grades and go down in other grades. During October 2020, it happened on the 1893-S, 1895, 1896-S, 1897-S, 1898, 1898-S, 1899-O, 1900-O, 1902-O, 1902-S, 1903-O, 1904 and the 1905-O. That is a fair amount of price changes and volatility in a small snapshot of a single series like Barber quarters.

Since prices move in a random fashion you must be aware of which coins are going up and which are static or going down. Having that knowledge and applying it to your purchases is the key to your success.

LEARN TO GRADE

Another facet of coin collecting education is learning to grade coins. Start with the series that you want to collect. Read all of the grading books that you can find. Look online at the PCGS and NGC websites where coins in different grades are depicted. STUDY THEM. But do not get discouraged. Grading coins takes years to perfect. It is an ART and not a SCIENCE and subjective things such as eye-appeal and toning affect the coin's grade and price. It will become a labor of love to learn to grade but it is well worth it. If you cannot grade those coins accurately, then we **strongly suggest** that you only buy NGC or PCGS graded coins, until you are more expert in grading.

And going to a coin show and looking at hundreds (or thousands) of NGC or PCGS graded coins is a great exercise. It helps you learn how the grading services look at and grade coins. But don't get discouraged. Every series is different and offers its own challenges. So take it slow and learn to grade—series by series. Copper coins are graded differently than silver or gold coins are due to the hardness of the metals and when they were graded. Grading of 18th century coins is more liberal than coins struck in the 20th century. As the technology improved the grading standards got tougher.

Also, the American Numismatic Association (www.money.org) offers grading classes in July at their Summer Seminar (https://www.money.org/summer-seminar) where two weeks of different classes are offered. These classes are also offered at some large coin shows. We all highly recommend taking an ANA grading course or all three of them (Beginning – Intermediate – Advanced). They offer courses for beginners as well as advanced collectors. Attending classes at the ANA will help your confidence as well as your collection to grow.

SELECT YOUR DEALER, AS YOU WOULD YOUR COINS—CAREFULLY!

Selecting a dealer to work with is no easy process. Sometimes a dealer may want to force his ideas (and inventory) on you. That should be red flag for you. The key to selecting a dealer is getting one who LISTENS to you. He (or she) is the expert, but YOU are the customer. It is your money you are spending, so make certain the dealer answers your questions completely. Make certain that the dealer is available for you when you have questions. Make certain that the dealer is giving you good advice.

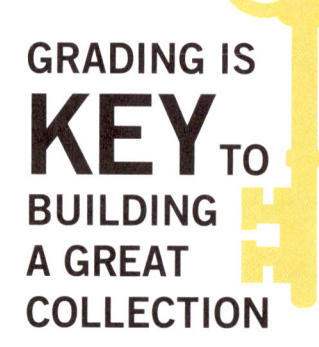

Now the dealer needs to make a profit to stay in business. You should not negotiate on every coin all of the time. If the dealer doesn't make a profit and has to fight you on every price, while his other clients listen to him and only push back a little bit, who do you think is going to get the BEST deals? Who do you think is going to get "first shot" (first chance) at his coins in the future?

People enjoy doing business with people that they like. Have you ever been to a coin show and seen one dealer fighting (in a good natured way) with another dealer over price? And then the show closes and the discussion between the two fighting dealers is "where are we going to eat dinner?" Why would you want to go to dinner with someone who fights with you over prices? BECAUSE YOU ARE FRIENDS!

Using your knowledge to get a better price from a dealer is not a crime, but understand who that dealer is. Is he someone who takes "shots" at you—meaning he throws out a very high price expecting

> GRADING IS
> **KEY** TO
> BUILDING
> A GREAT
> COLLECTION

that you will always make a counter-offer? Or is he someone who adds a modest profit and wants to sell it quickly? Knowing what a coin should be worth is your starting point. If the coin is Greysheet bid at $1,000 and the dealer quotes you $1,150 or so, he is likely making a modest profit and trying to build a relationship with you. He wants your business. He wants you as a customer.

If the dealer is asking $1,500 for that coin that bids for $1,000, is he asking too much? Well, that depends on whether he had to pay more than the Greysheet bid price in order to get the coin. Is the Greysheet always right? Yes and No. It may be correct that the dealer has not upped their price from $1,000 but all of the dealers at the show want $1,500 for their coin. No pricing guide is always correct for every coin in every grade—especially when you are publishing a couple of hundred thousand prices! So, in that instance, what do you do?

(Most transactions today at coin shows seem to be dealer-to-dealer. Photo courtesy of author.)

You like the coin, you like how it looks, it's well struck, and it has nice eye-appeal—but is it over-priced? There is only one way to find that out. Look on the Heritage or Stacks website for previous auction comps—auction comparable prices. Look at other dealers' tables for the same date, mintmark, grade and grading service. Are they all around $1,500—then the Greysheet bid is too low.

Use common sense—if a deal seems too good to be true—it likely is! There are no "free lunches" in the coin business.

The coin dealer you select should be there to help you. Ask him lots of questions about the typical strike or the availability of certain coins. A good dealer wants to answer your questions and wants to help you.

Your dealer can and should be helpful to you. Avoid dealers that want you to buy quickly and those who do not listen and respond to your questions or concerns.

But you need to be easy to deal with and follow through when you commit to buy something. If you don't, you might need to look for a new dealer.

One other thing—avoid coins with problems. I know this is controversial and some dealers might disagree, but coins with problems are just that—PROBLEM COINS! The problems don't go away. They don't get better with time. Buying a cleaned AU graded coin, in my opinion, is not as attractive or as easily salable as selling a matching set of nice, problem-free XF coins.

JOIN THE CLUB!

Joining a local coin club as well as the ANA and other regional clubs is a great way to learn your hobby and series. Many coin club meetings are generally well attended by older, more veteran collectors. If you are new to the hobby, most collectors will welcome you to the hobby. As you get to know them ask them questions and they will try to help you. The collectors there will help you learn and introduce you to local dealers. Not only are you supporting the hobby but you are also improving your knowledge. Going to coin shows and attending meetings held at large regional coin shows of various clubs allows you to learn about the coins they all collect and helps you to make friends in the hobby.

The coin hobby is very social. So get involved. But be careful. Keep your address private. Don't brag about your collection to strangers. Be careful and as you get to know people, they will open up more and you can too. But take it slow and easy. Be careful!

RECORD-KEEPING, BUDGETS, INSURANCE, STORAGE

Recordkeeping can be easy or hard depending on what type of a person you are. You can make it easy. As you start to buy coins, use Excel or any spreadsheet or inventory program. Make certain to keep your purchase receipts, assign each coin an inventory number, date of purchase, description, grade and cost (add any fields that you like—date purchased, date sold, quantity, dealer, etc.) and keep track of your collection. This may not be incredibly important to you because you might remember what you paid for a certain coin. But what about your spouse or kids? How will they know what you paid for something? How will they know one coin is worth 10x, 20x, 100x what the others are worth? The answer is—they wouldn't. So do it for them! Keep good records and also give them some direction. A modest collection can be sold outright. A more expensive collection might garner the best results once it is at auction. As your collection grows, think about what would happen if you weren't there to sell it!

Budgets are very easy to set but very difficult to keep. It is very easy to overspend. Especially at the start of a collection, it's easy to want to buy everything. Well—you can't! Set goals and do not overspend your budget. The easiest thing to do at a coin show is spend money. One of the hardest things is to get a good value. Look at the coins. Study their grade. Look at their prices. And verify that the price is correct. Spend your money carefully. Look at lots of coins, talk to lots of dealers, and then spend your money. You will be happy that you did.

One of the many benefits of being a member of the American Numismatic Association is that members are offered inexpensive coin collection insurance that is much cheaper than a rider on your homeowner's policy.

https://www.money.org/uploads/Public%20ANA%20Member%20Benefits%20Guide.pdf

Keeping your collection, or parts of it anyway, in your local bank's safe deposit boxes is a great way to keep it safe and secure. For a collection that you are currently actively working on it is inconvenient. But for something you just want to store safely, it's hard to beat those bank safe deposit box fees and your collection insurance becomes even more inexpensive when stored in a bank safe deposit box.

For a collection that you are currently working on, a gun safe or other large safe makes a great deterrent in case your home is broken into. Having your valuable collection in two different places decreases the odds of total loss through robbery, fire, flood or tornado.

If storing your collection in a safe in your home, keep a low profile and only tell the people who need to know what is in there and where it is stored. The fewer people who know you have a collection and where it is stored—the better.

BUYING AT COIN SHOWS

(A massive Florida United Numismatists (FUN) coin show with more than 1,000 dealers available. Photo courtesy of The Florida United Numismatists [FUN].)

Coin shows and conventions are great places to buy or sell coins, meet dealers and fellow collectors.

You made it to one of the largest coin shows in the country. Every dealer who is anybody is there. The major collectors are there. Several large auction houses are vying with the 1,000 dealers for your attention and for your money.

The benefits of buying at a coin show:

- Lots of dealers and inventory there
- Compare inventories and prices

- Get second opinions on your contemplated purchases
- Dealers are often more competitive at shows, price-wise, due to the competition.

The downside to buying at a coin show:

- So much competition—where do you start?
- Comparing prices for similar coins can take hours—or days even
- The lighting may not be the best at a show or at a dealer's table
- Are you feeling pressure to buy while sitting at a dealer's table and taking up his valuable time and real estate at the show?

Overall, I believe that buying at a coin show can be a good thing. Take your time. Be careful. Research the prices. And show the coin, if possible, to get another opinion.

SHOULD YOU BUY COINS AT AUCTION?

I think as you gain more experience buying at auction is something that you should try. But remember this. It is VERY EASY to get caught up in the excitement of bidding at auction. Also remember this—the auction company will add 15% to 25% to the winning bid as their commission. Suddenly, a $250 coin you "ripped at auction for $200" is now over $250 due to commissions and sales taxes, if any.

Do your homework. Look at the auction lots carefully. Write down a price that you are willing to bid for that exact coin on your auction catalog and stick to that price! Do not keep upping your bid. It is easy to pay too much at auction.

Get your auction catalog at home and do your research there. Check rarity, price, and the coin's provenance or history. Study the catalog images. Spend your time doing that work at home so you won't have to do it at the show. Then at the show, in the auction suite, just study the actual coin and simply check the current prices.

Make sure you know how much additional the auction company will charge as the buyer's premium (their fee) and factor that into your price estimate. Don't keep upping your bid as other coins get away from you. Stick with the price you want to pay. But don't expect it will be a steal. With so many collectors and dealers there, it should bring a fair price! Good luck and have fun!

HOW TO NEGOTIATE BETTER PRICES

You are walking around at a coin show and suddenly you stop! There it is! A coin that you have been looking for—show after show. It is just sitting there quietly... inside your heart is pounding faster and faster. You want to add it to your collection, but you want a good deal. Are those two desires—buying the coin at all costs and getting a good deal on it—incompatible?

No they aren't! Okay, so what is the trick? How do you do it? After 40 years as a coin dealer, I think that I can help you.

There are my 10 rules for you to follow:

1. **Be friendly** – Every coin dealer would rather deal with someone who is a "nice person." You are always more willing to deal with someone who is nice. Say hello. Be polite. You feel better and you make a good impression on the dealer. I would also give the exact same advice to the dealer. Why should a buyer deal with a grouchy coin dealer? But YOU can start the friend-fest rolling! Be friendly.

2. **Be aware** – If the dealer is involved in talking to other collectors or other dealers, acknowledge him and just quickly tell him you will be back. If he is truly busy, he will appreciate it. Interrupting him might annoy him, if you need his attention on a $100 coin, when he is discussing a $10,000 deal. If his conversations are social rather than business, this will give him at opportunity to break off the social chat and do some business, which is why he is at the show to begin with.

WHAT COLLECTORS & INVESTORS NEED TO KNOW

3. **Be knowledgeable** – If you know what the current Greysheet price is then mention it to him. It allows the dealer to understand where the "wholesale" market is. He likely paid the Greysheet wholesale bid or a little more or a little less for his coin that you want to buy. But know that there are exceptions. Some coins trade for much more or for less than the printed wholesale price. It is not always accurate but it is 80–90% of the time.

   Expect the dealer to want to make a profit on it as well—that is how dealers stay in business. On a bullion coin—5% or less is not unreasonable. On a collector coin—10 to 20% is normal. On a really rare coin, or one that has amazing toning, expect to pay a LOT more. Likely the dealer paid a LOT more for that special coin too!

4. **Don't be afraid to negotiate** – Some dealers tell you "this is my best price" and often they mean it. They may not be able to lower the price because they do not own the coin outright—they might own half the coin and he is partners with someone else. But he might also own the coin and have had it in inventory for some time. Some dealers take "shots" at a customer—they throw out a high price and hope you want the coin more than anything and that you are uncomfortable negotiating. Ask, "what is your absolute best price on this coin," and see what he says. If it is a good price look at the coin again and then either commit to buy it or thank him and move on. Too many times a collector is given a good price and they are afraid to pull the trigger and buy it. They often lose that special well-priced coin to another collector.

5. **Do not over-negotiate** – He quoted you a very fair price for the coin. Coming back with a counter-offer sometimes works if the dealer is desperate to sell it. But if you both

know it is a good price, over-negotiating makes the dealer think you are one-sided. For a deal to work, it has to be good for both parties. Do not get greedy.

6. **Do you take cash?** – Some dealers love to take cash as payment. For some of the larger dealers it is more of a hassle. If the dealer prefers cash you have a little additional leverage. If he doesn't want cash, or if you don't have enough cash, you may have to give him a check. Remember, you have his coin. All he is getting in return is a piece of paper that is a promise to pay, do not feel offended is he asks other dealers about you—has this guy ever bounced a check to you, is his reputation good? Expect it. Remember many dealers, especially those at smaller shows are part-time dealers and cannot afford losses. So they are exceedingly careful. Carrying cash, if safe to do so, is a good method to getting good prices. Sometimes a dealer will sell a coin for $25–$50 less for cash.

7. **Don't ask for terms AFTER you agree to buy it** – You found a nice coin, you negotiated the best price. Then you want to ask the dealer if he could hold your check for 2 weeks, until you get paid again. Suddenly, the deal that the dealer thought he had, now changes. That is not fair nor should you expect him to accept the "new terms" with a smile. He might accept it—he may not. It depends on his financial situation. In any event, if there are any terms with your payment tell the dealer upfront. Dealers always try to be more accommodating when they know your situation before negotiations begin.

8. **Buyer's remorse** – You buy a coin at a coin show. It isn't perfect. But it is nice, fairly priced and close to the grade that you want. As you walk around the show, you see the PERFECT coin. It is the exact grade you want and it is fairly

priced. You want to buy it but you don't want two of them. Now what do you do?

What I would suggest is to go back to the dealer you bought the first coin from and explain what happened. Do NOT expect the coin dealer to simply give you your money back, no questions asked! He isn't Walmart! Ask him if he would like to buy it back at a lower price than you paid. Many times he may want to do that. If you paid $225 for a coin, offer it back to him at $190–200. Yes, you lose a little bit of money but you keep a dealer connection and he knows you recognize that he needs a profit to stay in business.

9. **Buy what you like and what you know**   I have been at coin shows where collectors come up and 5 out of 10 of them will ask for the same type of coins. Everyone is chasing the "hot coins" or the "hot series" in the market. So, you buy it and eventually the buyers stop buying. Guess what happens? Prices fall. You are better off buying what you know and like than chasing the hot commodity of the month. If you buy coins that YOU like, YOU will always enjoy owning them. It is a better way to enjoy our hobby than any other I know. Don't be talked into buying something you don't really like or understand. Make up your own mind and you will be much happier.

10. **Be a familiar face** – Back when I was much younger I would go to 6 to 8 coin shows a month. I would see hundreds of collectors at these shows. As I got to know some of them, then knew I was someone they could trust. I got to know them and know what they liked/collected and how reliable they were. I also got to know who had a "good check." These were the collectors I tried to always give good deals to, because I know I would be rewarded with their future business.

Remember, you are at a coin show. Go slowly. Find a nice coin that you really like. Study its price and it's recent price history.

Take your time. Great collections aren't built overnight. They take years to assemble in most instances, sometimes decades! But think of all of the fun and friendships you will make while assembling your great collection!

11 | TO DEAL OR NOT TO DEAL?

This chapter is truly for aspiring coin dealers. So you want to be a coin dealer? It involves lots of hard work, studying, traveling and making deals. Sometimes you will have more money than you have ever had. Other times you will have more coins, and little money, than you have ever had. But it is a great life! You are constantly learning. If you have a deep appreciation for U.S. history, or Canadian history or Roman history for that matter, you can use it to your advantage. You will learn so much about history, the law, our money, politics, economics, etc.—that no one in your family will ever want to play Trivial Pursuit or Jeopardy with you ever again. Seriously!

There are so many things for you to learn and to enjoy but let's get some good advice from our four friendly dealers who doled out great advice to collectors and investors. Tell us, what advice would you give to a new coin dealer starting out?

Jim Carr – "Be careful. Don't try to know everything at once. It takes years or decades to know 'a lot' about rare coins. Specialize. Learn about what you like. Go to coin shows. Go to coin clubs. Help people with advice. Share your knowledge. But be careful.

A PO Box in a different nearby city helps keep you safe by not letting people know where you live. Be cautious, especially at or going to or from coin shows. Be aware of your surroundings. Inside the coin show, take checks, only with good, strong references. Any collector or dealer can see their finances change but make the effort. Ask for references and check them out.

Treat collectors and Young Numismatists well. I always bring older Red Books (A Guide Book of United States Coins) to coin shows and give them to kids who attend the shows and are just starting out. You are adding to the longevity of the hobby in that way.

Remember—Your word is your bond. Avoid making enemies in this business, if you can.

Security is very important so get a PO in a different city. Keep your home and office addresses private.

Don't bounce a check. It will kill your reputation and find a bank that will work with you.

Be presentable—look your best."

Kevin Lipton – offers this advice to young dealers: "A young dealer starting out would be best served by fishing in 'smaller ponds'. Travel around to smaller coin shops and shows to try and buy there. Be friendly and make sure your checks are always good!

In order to have a 'long run' in the coin business, relationships are key. Make friends and always make sure to follow through on your commitments even if not in your best interests all the time. You will not make money on every transaction you do. Some of my best learning experiences were on deals I lost money on.

Be wary of extending credit to people without knowing 100% for sure that they are worthy. Just because a dealer is at a show doesn't mean his check will cash. Don't be afraid to ask for references and make sure to check them out.

Be knowledgeable about what you are selling. And share that knowledge with your customers. Write an article or three for your local coin club. If they have a newsletter or a website, I am sure they will appreciate your contribution. That sharing of your knowledge is very important.

You should ease into the business slowly. Start attending a few smaller shows, bringing some coins in a briefcase and walking around the 'bourse floor.' Some other points to remember are:

- Develop a budget. Do not overspend.
- Find a mentor.
- Be well organized.
- Be reasonable honest and fair.
- It is not an easy job—long hours sometimes for little pay. Education comes at a price"

You will start to hear some of the same pearls of wisdom over and over again. That's because every dealer learned them and they all want to make sure that YOU learn them too! There is some repetition here—but that means that all of these experienced dealers really want you to follow these suggestions so you can be successful.

Tom Caldwell – advises that you: "Find a mentor. Find another dealer who can and wants to teach you the ropes. Someone that can introduce you to all aspects of what it takes to become a successful dealer from the ground up. There is nothing like a hands-on in-the-trenches experience. You may very well come away from this experience with a particular area of numismatics that you wish to specialize in.

I strongly suggest that a young dealer or collector of any age consider attending the ANA summer seminar at the ANA headquarters in Colorado Springs multiples times. (Suspended in 2020 due to COVID.) You will have a choice of difference classes to choose from, including grading, photography, counterfeits, problem coins, ancient coins, paper money and more. You will learn from experts in the field who generously donate their time to help promote numismatics. Some scholarships for Young Numismatists are offered. Go to www.money.org/ANA-Summer-Seminar-Scholarships for more information.

There is typically a coin show in Colorado Springs during one of the summer seminar sessions. When they do safely start back up, you should attend. You can learn a lot talking to other dealers and by making some purchases and sales. You will probably make a mistake or two, but this can and should translate into a good learning experience. You will soon learn which dealers are helpful, encouraging, and willing to take the time with you.

To have longevity and success in this business, you must be willing to put in the time. Shows extend into weekends, so you will no doubt give up many hours and days that may otherwise be leisure time.

A lot of coin business is done online. We strongly advise getting an online presence right from the start. Start your own website, get involved in social media, see if eBay fits into your business plan, and explore any other online opportunities you can think of. You may be surprised how you can often compete with the big boys if you have a solid online presence.

To be a successful dealer, it would be beneficial to learn as many areas of numismatics that you can. Even if you decide to pursue a specialty, you will be presented with buying opportunities of all types of coins and it is important to take advantage of these opportunities. Perhaps California Fractional Gold, English Crowns, or Russian Rubles are not your area of expertise; however, you are in business to make money and a basic knowledge in these areas or at least learning how to handle them when presented with such coins will be important.

As you advance your career, be respectful of other dealers and also your customers. Treating people right goes a long way and can pay dividends in the end, and besides, it's the right thing to do. Reputation and integrity are crucial.

Lastly—Be Resilient!—the coin market inevitably goes through many phases throughout the years. What's popular today may not be in a month or two. In Northeast's well over half a century in business, we have seen it all."

Finally, **Gregg Hannigan** – made these suggestions to help you: "Becoming a dealer, whether it is full-time or part-time is not easy; be knowledgeable about the coins you are selling and always keep your word and be honest. Surround yourself with other dealers that have a great reputation.

Start attending the smaller coin shows first but definitely attend coin shows and start selling online as well. Coin Cube Trading is an amazing place to get started as well.

Become a student of the hobby, research the history and the cost of what you want to buy, and look at historical values before you jump into anything. Develop a budget and do not over spend it—this may be the most important thing to do. I have seen many dealers start off doing shows who were not on top of this and only lasted a couple of years in the industry because they were under-capitalized.

Find a mentor, I have two or three that I started becoming friends with, and make sure you surround yourself with class and the best people in the room—that's very important.

Be organized and supply your customers with a coin's provenance when you can and give your customers great service. Make sure you are kind and friendly all the time, even if you are having a bad day—remember—customers come first.

Attending coin club meetings and coin shows is very important as is joining the ANA, EAC if you love large cents coppers. Also join local coin clubs and when you can, try to become a Life Member—it supports your club.

Take notes during auctions and do not overreach and spend too much. Get to know the larger auction houses and all the folks running the local and regional coin shows.

Volunteer and be active in the coin community.

One other thing to consider is that I think selling online has a huge advantage in reducing your overspending and cost of attending coin shows.

Honestly and integrity is so important to anyone, especially a coin dealer. Be reasonable honest and fair.

Look, becoming a coin dealer is not always easy and the education does sometimes come at a cost. Some coin purchases fall through, and others do not always keep their value. Be careful and kind to your fellow dealers and be courteous to the dealers around you and offer help to them when you can,—this will go a long way towards them wanting to help you."

There is 200 years of accumulated numismatic dealer experience for you! Read it, study it, live by it!

Becoming a coin dealer guarantees you a moderately interesting life.

One other subject I would like to brooch is finances. Because there is always a temptation to try to buy every deal that is offered to you, resist that temptation. Once you are cash-poor and coin-rich you will find that you will be forced to sell coins too quickly and too cheaply. You need capital to be able to grow your business.

Working with a bank that understands the vagaries of the coin business is a great idea. The larger banks may not want to take the time to understand coin shows, bullion price movements, etc. But smaller banks, to which you would be a larger customer, just might be willing to look at your business, assign a bank officer to try to understand it and assign you the necessary lines of credit to allow you to sell coins for what they are worth and that would allow you to stop continually having to sell off your coins for tiny, fast profits. Sell your coins for what they are truly worth, but do not be greedy.

Look at several banks, open accounts with them. See which one will take an interest in you and will partner with you to help your business and their business to grow right along with you!

It takes some looking but they are out there. You just need to find one.

As for me, well I have my own rules for becoming a successful coin dealer. There are ten of them and they can work if you apply yourself.

TEN RULES FOR BEING A SUCCESSFUL COIN DEALER

1. **Read and research:** Think you know a lot? Well, being an expert in a single area of numismatics is great but it is very, very risky! Your area of expertise may go out of favor, or the market may get flooded with more of your favorite products than it can absorb. Lots of things can happen to YOUR market. It is much better to be a well-rounded numismatist, who isn't afraid of buying bullion, or gold coins, or silver dollars, or type coins, or exonumia, or currency, or world coins, or ancients. The more you know about various areas of our industry, the better off you will be.

2. **Go to coin shows:** Think you know what is going on in the coin market? You don't, unless you are at coin shows week in and week out. Fantastic auctions happen at coin shows and if you don't go to shows, you find out where the new price levels are, well after the fact. Shows are also great places to learn the latest employment moves, gossip and rumors in the coin business. Start locally, then regionally, then a major, then all of the majors. You will be well-informed by going to these shows. And you will meet dealers who live across the country who will become your life-long friends and trading partners. You will make lots of money dealing with people who become your friends—what a great life!

3. **Technology is your friend:** Not every technological innovation is great but most will help you be more efficient and smarter. I remember people negatively and quizzically commenting on Jim Halperin's repeated purchase of computers in the very early 1980 for New England Rare Coin Galleries. Most dealers had no idea why Jim would do that. But most dealers didn't know how much technology would help them. Today, having every technological bell and whistle isn't required to be successful but leveraging the

technology that you can use and understand is important. It is required if you want to compete and survive. Will that iPad or Surface Pro help you make better buys? If your buying and selling history is in your database, it certainly can. Technology can make you smarter. Use it! It is your friend.

4. **Borrow—lightly:** Okay. You go to a major national coin show. I guarantee you that at least one major auction house is there—maybe all of them are there. And one of them is holding that show's official auction. The Consignment Directors get to know the dealers who are spending money in their auctions. But they also would like you to spend a little bit more too. So, they offer you some "AHC" (Auction House Credit). It starts out slowly but as you pay it back within 30 days they offer you a bit more and a bit more. It is a great way to conserve the money in your business checking account and use the AHC to buy new coins at the auction. In a market like 1985–89 you can make a fortune using the auction company's money. But there is a catch to it—the auction houses want you to pay back the amount that they lent you, with interest! The auction companies get a little upset when you don't. Seriously, if you are bad with using your credit cards—avoid AHC. If you are good with credit it can really help you extend your ability to buy. But I have seen dealers buy too much at auctions and 25 days after the auction, they are selling auction "newps" at under what they paid for them just to raise the cash that they need to pay back the auction house. It is a great option but use it wisely.

5. **Get a mentor:** A mentor can help you—they know what to tell you to do, they can help you by teaching you "the ropes" at a particular coin show so you don't look foolish, they can introduce you to other good dealers, and they can vouch for you financially. Having a mentor is extremely

helpful. But only if you learn from them. They can tell you about the mistakes that they made so you don't make those same ones. But you've got to listen. Most importantly, their introducing you to other dealers is critical. Older dealers love to mentor younger dealers. Most, older dealers realize that YOU are the future of our business, so they want to help you. Many younger dealers have embraced technology far better than we old-timers so you can help your mentor at times. That bonding relationship will help you grow and help you grow your business. It is critically important to find someone who will become your mentor. But if you cannot, many dealers will still answer your questions and help you as much as they feel comfortable doing. Look for someone with a great reputation and a dealer that most people like. That person is a perfect choice to be your mentor because some day you will want to be him.

6. **Your word is your bond:** In our industry, if you say you will buy something, you go and do it. If you promise to sell something to someone at a particular price, you do it. Once you make a promise, if you do not keep it, how can you be trusted in the future? Our industry has survived on people keeping their word, YOU must do the same. Otherwise, you will not be fully trusted and you will not be fully accepted. This is probably the most important rule on this list. Make certain not to promise anything that you cannot follow through on.

Now mistakes will happen. You might mis-speak. But if your word has been good up until that point in time, your dealer friends will be very forgiving. Sometimes you will speak first and think about it afterwards—maybe that wasn't a smart thing to promise. Still, if you gave your word, follow through. There may be some financial consequences but they are less important than how your future promises are received. Don't give your word easily; ask yourself do I really want to buy/do that? But once you have made a promise, you must follow through. If you don't, it will be hard for people to trust you in the future.

7. **Live within your means:** Sounds simple but many people, including coin dealers, do not. They try to buy anything and everything rather than what they know they can make money on. Most importantly do not bounce a check. If you aren't good at staying within your budgeted amount get overdraft protection at your bank. But once you bounce a check, especially to your friends, they will forgive you but they will always worry about your check. And coin dealers love to talk so a bounced check may make you the subject of much undesirable conversation.

   Sometimes, you take a check from a larger dealer, who should be better capitalized, than you are and it suddenly bounces. Now your check bounces and likely so do the checks of a number of other smaller dealers. While that sometimes cannot be avoided, the best way to handle it is to be the guy who shares that information with the dealers that you affected. They would rather hear the whole story from you than from their bank. Break the bad news to them first and your dealer friends will be much more forgiving.

8. **Learn to say NO:** Everyone has a financial limit. Some have modest limits, some have extravagant limits. Remember this fact: YOU CAN'T BUY EVERYTHING. Not every deal is a good deal. Some are better than others. When you are starting out some other dealers may try to dump their slow-moving inventory on you. Be careful. Know what you want to buy. Stick to your plan. Only buy what you think is a good deal—whether it is from another dealer or a retail customer. Smart dealers save their money for coins they know they can sell or for coins too cheap to pass up.

Another basic tenet to learn: **QUANTITY KILLS**. You might be able to sell three 1938-D Buffalo Nickels for $65 each, that you bought for $45 each. But if someone wants to sell you 30 coins at $30 each do you buy them? Well, history has shown me that large quantities spell trouble. Unless you have access to lots of dealers who will buy quantity avoid large quantities of anything. Large deals that are a good mix of dates/products are fine. Quantities of the same item can be deadly—be careful.

9. **Treat young collectors well:** Just as you are the future of the coin dealer industry, young collectors are the future of the hobby. They are starting to love coins. They are starting to see how much fun this hobby is. It is up to you to help them, encourage them, and spend time with them. They need encouragement and seeing younger dealers makes them realize that someday, they could be you. You are important ambassadors of dealers to the next generation of collectors. And these young collectors may grow up to be good customers as they get older and have more money. As we are trying to help you learn our industry rules, you can help them learn what to collect and what is fun to own. Always encourage them to collect what THEY like.

10. **All markets are cyclical:** Gold goes up, silver dollars go down, and commemoratives go sideways. The markets change all the time. What is popular and rising today may turn around and give back profits tomorrow. Remember that! No market always just goes up or just goes down. Every market is cyclical. Including the financial markets. You are a relatively new dealer at a coin show. Many of the more experienced dealers will come by to see what you have and to see how much you know. Then the collectors will start to come in the door. To many of them, YOU are the expert. You know more than they do. The stock market

is flying high. A collector asks you if you were him, would you take money out of the stock market to buy coins. What would you say? You can remind him that ALL markets are cyclical. You can remind him that his mutual funds will not always only go up. You can remind him that diversification is critically important to his financial success.

PREPARING FOR COIN SHOWS

Preparing to attend a coin show is an important part of life for the average coin dealer. This checklist will help you get ready for the show and not to forget completing any important tasks. The form is set up so you know when to start a task and by what date it must be completed. Using this checklist as a guide create your own checklist—and use it!

COIN SHOW CHECKLIST:

Name of Show: _____

Dates: _____

Location: _____

Attendees: _____

_____

_____

_____

_____

_____

_____

_____

3 Months Prior:

Date: _____

Table(s) Secured: [ ] Yes

Number(s): _____

Memberships Needed: _____

Badges Needed: _____

Safe Rental: [ ] Yes

From: _____

Size: _____

Hotel Reservations [ ] Yes

Hotel: _____

1 – 2 Months Prior:

Date: _____

Flights Secured [ ] Yes

Comment: _____

Have Sufficient Checks [ ] Yes

Comment: _____

Have Sufficient Invoices [ ] Yes

Comment: _____

Customer Consignments [ ] Yes

Comment: _____

Inventory Flipped & Ready [ ] Yes

Comment: _____

1 Week Prior:

Date: _____

Shipping Supplies to Show [ ] Yes

Comment: _____

Obtain UPS/USPS/FedEx Labels [ ] Yes

Comment: _____

Inventory [ ] Yes

Have a complete inventory list w/ID numbers and Costs.

1 Day Prior:

Date: _____

Pack Everything [ ] Yes

Comment: _____

Everything Checked [ ] Yes

Comment: _____

At Show:

Date: _____

Supplies Needed [ ] Yes

Comment: _____

Booth Setup [ ] Yes

Comment: _____

Daily Activities:

Date(s): _____

Checks Recorded [ ] Yes

Comment: _____

Packages Picked up [ ] Yes

Comment: _____

Inventory Secured Nightly [ ] Yes

Comment: In Safe   At Table   In Security Room   (circle one)

Inventory Secured Nightly [ ] Yes

Comment: In Safe   At Table   In Security Room   (circle one)

Inventory Secured Nightly [ ] Yes

Comment: In Safe   At Table   In Security Room   (circle one)

Inventory Secured Nightly [ ] Yes

Comment: In Safe   At Table   In Security Room   (circle one)

Inventory Secured Nightly [ ] Yes

Comment: In Safe   At Table   In Security Room   (circle one)

SECURITY CONSIDERATIONS

Traveling to coin shows all across the country sounds like a great deal of fun. Traveling to exotic locations. Traveling to nice weather areas during winter. Boy! Coin dealers have a fantastic and glamorous life!

Well not really! Yes you travel a lot—but this isn't for vacation or fun. It's for you to work 12–16 hour days, and for you to risk your own money on buying coins that you HOPE will sell. But you are doing something that you truly love. And many times that offsets all of the risks.

But travel today is full of risks. Traveling with valuables is never easy or fun. So you must be careful, quiet and on guard at all times while you are traveling. Here is a list of rules to follow while you are traveling to keep you, and your valuable cargo safe and secure.

You are traveling on behalf of your company. It is important that you travel professionally, safely and wisely.

BEFORE THE SHOW:
1. Your airline reservations should be complete and secure.
2. Your hotel accommodations should be complete and secure.
3. Ground travel is often an afterthought so make certain you can get from the airport to the hotel and back easily.

TRAVELING TO THE SHOW:
1. Keep copies of all expenses and ask for receipts at all times. If you cannot obtain a receipt, write down the expense accurately.
2. When traveling, do not wear any clothing with your company name or the name of any coin company, grading service or other coin vendor. Do not bring unwanted attention to yourself.
3. Since you will be carrying inventory with you, ask for a TSA private screening so that no one knows that you are carrying valuables.
4. Travel in groups is the safest possible way. Be very aware of your surroundings.
5. Do not speak loudly about the "coin show" or "gold" etc.
6. If traveling between hotels and convention centers, Uber and Lyft are acceptable means of transportation and cheaper than taxis. If carrying large amounts of products, renting a vehicle may be your safest method.
7. Try never to check any of your valuables—coins, checks, laptops, iPads, etc. with the airline. You might never see them again. It is safer to carry them on the plane with you.
8. If carrying coins to the airport, place them in a clear, heavy duty, plastic bag, which makes it much easier for TSA to see what is in the bag during your private screening. Do not touch any of the coins once TSA is to inspect your bag. Let them tell you when it is okay for you to touch your property once again.

9. It is helpful to have a story ready so that when an Uber driver or taxi driver casually asks why you are in town, you have a reason that does not draw attention to you and the fact that you are carrying valuables.

AT THE COIN SHOW:
1. Make certain that you have a written inventory of all of your valuables, including certified numbers on the slabbed coins.
2. On any particularly valuable coins, take photos of them in their slabs with your phone so you have proof of the coins, for identification purposes.
3. Google your travel routes, if attending a show where you are unfamiliar with the routes to be taken. This will prevent someone from taking you to an unsafe area.
4. Try to travel with others to the show, convention center or hotel. There is safety in numbers.
5. At the show, do not sell anything until you are completely set up. You do not want to be distracted while setting up.
6. Set up your inventory with the more valuable items in harder to reach places inside the showcases.
7. Set up the inventory so that it is easy to see if something is missing. If your coins are in trays inside a showcase do not stack the coins. Make it easy to see what may be missing.
8. Deal with only one customer (per person) at a time. Focus on where your inventory is at all times.
9. Small video cameras are very inexpensive, can easily be mounted on your cases and they discourage theft.
10. Always LOCK your showcase and do NOT leave the keys in the locks. Take them with you at all times.
11. Remember what coins are being shown to which customers and look at the coins you are receiving back to ensure that they have not been switched for a similar coin. Writing down the coin description takes only seconds and discourages theft.

12. Do not store cash where it can be easily seen and tempt someone.
13. If possible, store your inventory in locked briefcases in the security room as opposed to locked showcases on your table.
14. Remove your badge when you leave the bourse floor for the evening.
15. If you are updating your inventory at the show, take a photo with your phone of the updated inventory list.

RETURNING FROM THE SHOW:
1. Make sure everything is safely packed. Remember you will need to deal with TSA/airport security once more so make sure valuables are accessible but secure.
2. Get your boarding passes during the show as close to 24 hours prior to departure as possible. Set an alarm on your phone to remind you as you may be busy at your table or buying on the floor.
3. Take your time. Leave early so an unexpected travel delay doesn't affect your travel plans.
4. Leave with others for safety reasons.

A FEW FINAL THOUGHTS...

Most of us who have spent decades in the coin business wouldn't trade our lives for any other line of work. It's fun, it's enjoyable, and it's (usually) profitable.

While there is always risk, if you are vigilant and take your travel plans seriously and treat your time at the shows seriously, you can be very successful. Many young dealers will find their niche in the business fairly quickly. Be a good person and you will easily build great relationships that often last a lifetime.

Be friendly. You can learn a great deal just by listening. You can learn to be an important part of a great occupation that is nearly two hundred years old in this country.

Thanks for reading this book. I hope you found lots of important information in it.

I wish you all the best of luck!

Mike Garofalo